Betty Crocker's

GREAT CHICKEN RECIPES

MACMILLAN • USA

Macmillan General Reference
A Simon & Schuster Macmillan Company
1633 Broadway
New York, NY 10019-6785

Library of Congress Cataloging-in-Publication data

Crocker, Betty.
  [Great chicken recipes]
  Betty Crocker's great chicken recipes.
    p.   cm.
  Includes index.
  ISBN 0-02-861622-7
  1. Cookery (Chicken) I. Title. II. Title: Great chicken
recipes.
TX750.5.C45C75   1993
641.6'65—dc20   92-25398
                                                      CIP

Designed by Levavi & Levavi
Manufactured in the United States of America

          10 9 8 7 6 5

On the front cover: Gingered Chicken with Pea Pods (page 60)

Contents

Introduction

Just about everyone likes chicken—it's versatile, economical, low in fat, high in protein, and fits in well with a healthful eating plan. It's no wonder that new ways to prepare chicken are always welcome, as well as sure-fire recipes for comforting classics and tried-and-true favorites.

You'll find everything you need to know about chicken right here in this easy-to-use book. We begin by explaining chicken basics—what the different types of chicken are, how to store and freeze it safely, and how to cut up a whole chicken and bone a chicken breast. Next, all the techniques you need for cooking chicken are gathered for your convenience. Learn how to roast a chicken perfectly, make gravy, broil chicken in your oven or cook it oudoors, poach chicken for salads and other delicious recipes, and microwave chicken.

With these basics under your belt, sample the array of recipes in this collection, sure to fill the bill for all your chicken needs. Try tasty salads and sandwiches such as Chicken Barbecue Sandwiches and Thai Chicken Salad, and savory soups—Chicken Tortilla Soup or Mulligatawny, to name just a few.

Skillet dishes are great for quick suppers; try Chicken in Red Wine Vinegar, Spicy Chicken with Broccoli, Raspberry-Peach Chicken, or other delicious dishes. And, who doesn't enjoy the aroma of chicken cooking in the oven? With a whole chapter on oven entrees, you can choose from a wonderful range of great dishes, including Baked Chicken with Biscuits and Gravy, Moroccan Chicken with Olives, Five-Spice Chicken, and many more.

BETTY CROCKER'S GREAT CHICKEN RECIPES is a book you'll come back to again and again. Whether you are looking for the best recipe for a classic dish, basic information on how to cook chicken, or fresh ideas that will inspire family and friends, you'll find everything you need right here.

THE BETTY CROCKER EDITORS

Chicken Basics

Buying chicken can be confusing when you see the array of choices in your local market. The information below will help you to buy just the right chicken for your recipe. Then, once you have bought your chicken, follow the guidelines below to store it properly and safely. You'll also learn how to cut up a whole chicken and bone a chicken breast yourself at home—both ways to make chicken even more economical.

Broiler-fryer Chicken: This all-purpose chicken weighs from 3 to 3½ pounds, and your best bargain is buying the whole bird; the bigger the bird, the more meat in proportion to the bone. Allow about ½ pound (bone in) per serving. Cut-up chicken and boneless chicken parts, such as thighs and breasts, will cost more per pound, but offer greater convenience.

Roaster Chicken: This chicken is a little older and larger than the broiler-fryer, weighing 4 to 6 pounds, with tender meat that is well suited for roasting.

Stewing Chicken (hen): This chicken weighs 4½ to 6 pounds and provides a generous amount of meat. It is a mature, less tender bird and is best cooked by simmering or in stews and soups.

Rock Cornish Hen (game hen): Small, young, specially bred chickens, weighing 1 to 1½ pounds, these hens have all white meat. Allow ½ to 1 small hen per person. Most supermarkets carry frozen Cornish hens; however, your butcher may be able to special-order fresh hens.

COOKED POULTRY EQUIVALENTS

TYPE AND READY-TO-COOK WEIGHT	APPROXIMATE COOKED YIELD
3- to 4-pound broiler-fryer chicken	3 to 4 cups cubed chicken
4½- to 6-pound stewing chicken	4½ to 6 cups cubed chicken

STORING CHICKEN

Raw chicken: Tray-packed chicken should be stored in its original wrapping in the refrigerator. Chicken wrapped in meat-market paper should be rinsed with cold water, patted dry and repackaged in plastic bags, plastic wrap or food storage containers. Refrigerate for no longer than 2 days.

Cooked chicken: Cover or wrap cooked chicken tightly and refrigerate it for no longer than 2 days. Chicken, giblets, stuffing and gravy should be stored in separate containers.

FREEZING CHICKEN

Wrap raw or uncooked chicken tightly (not giblets—freeze them separately) in moisture-vapor-resistant freezer wrap, such as plastic freezer bags, freezer paper or heavy-duty aluminum foil. Press as much air as possible out of the package before sealing it. Mark the package with the date and then freeze.

Spoon casseroles or chicken in gravy or sauce into freezer containers with tight-fitting lids. (Casserole dishes that can be placed in the oven directly from the freezer are very handy.)

Cut-up cooked chicken should be frozen in broth to cover it, if it is to be stored for a month or longer. Do not stuff a chicken and freeze it for later roasting—always stuff chicken just before it is to be cooked.

MAXIMUM STORAGE TIMES AT 0° F	
CHICKEN	STORAGE TIME
Cooked	
Creamed or in broth	3 to 4 months
No sauce or broth	1 month
Uncooked	
Cut up	4 to 6 months
Giblets	1 to 3 months
Whole	6 to 8 months
Broth	2 to 3 months

Cutting Up a Whole Chicken

1. Place breast side up on a cutting surface. Remove wings by cutting into wing joint with a sharp knife, rolling knife to let the blade follow through at curve of the joint.

2. Remove legs by cutting skin between thigh and body; cut through meat between tail and hip joint. Bend leg back until hip joint pops out; cut around bone and through remaining meat and skin.

3. Separate drumsticks from thighs by cutting toward the drumstick at about ⅛ inch from the line of fat that runs crosswise between drumstick and thigh.

4. Cut breast from backbone by holding body, neck and end down, and cutting down along each side of the backbone through the rib joints.

5. Placing breasts with skin side down, cut just through white cartilage at V of neck to expose end of keel bone (the dark bone at center of breast).

6. Bend back both sides of the breast to pop out keel bone. Cut breasts into halves with knife or kitchen scissors. See illustration #2 (next page).

Boning a Chicken Breast

1. Remove skin from a whole chicken breast. Place meaty side down on a clean, dry cutting surface. Cut just through the white cartilage at the V of the neck to expose the end of the keel bone (the dark bone at the center of the breast.)

2. Bend the breast halves back until the keel bone pops away from the meat. Run a finger along each side of the keel bone to loosen it. Pull the bone out: if it comes out in pieces, that is fine.

3. To remove the rib cages, insert the point of the knife under the long rib bone. Cut the rib cage away from the meat. Cut through the shoulder joint to free the entire rib cage.

4. To cut away the wishbone, slip the knife under the white tendons on either side of the breast; loosen and pull out the tendons. Cut the breast into halves.

How to Use Nutrition Information

Nutrition Information Per Serving for each recipe includes the amounts of calories, protein, carbohydrate, fat, cholesterol and sodium.

- If ingredient choices are given, the first listed ingredient is used in recipe nutrition information calculations.

- When ingredient ranges or more than one serving size is indicated, the first weight or serving is used to calculate nutrition information.
- "If desired" ingredients and recipe variations are not included in nutrition information calculations.

SIMPLY GOOD CHICKEN RECIPES

The following recipes are classic, basic ways to cook chicken. You'll learn how to roast a chicken and make stuffing and gravy; poach chicken for salads or other recipes that require cooked chicken; broil or grill chicken; and how to use your microwave to cook chicken.

Roast Chicken

Remove giblets if present (gizzard, heart and neck). Rinse cavity. Rub cavity of bird lightly with salt if desired. Do not salt cavity if bird is to be stuffed. If stuffing is desired, stuff just before roasting—not ahead of time. (See Bread Stuffing on page ix.) Fill wishbone area with stuffing first. Fasten neck skin to back with skewer. Fold wings across back with tips touching. Fill body cavity lightly. (Do not pack—stuffing will expand while cooking.) Tuck drumsticks under band of skin at tail, or tie or skewer to tail.

Place bird, breast side up, on rack in shallow roasting pan. Brush with melted margarine or butter. Do not add water. Do not cover. Follow Timetable for Roasting (below) for approximate roasting time. There is no substitute for a meat thermometer for determining doneness—place in thigh muscle, so thermometer does not touch bone.

Roast until juices run clear (no pink should remain). Whole birds should reach an internal temperature of 180° when done and the drumstick should move easily when lifted or twisted.

Calories per cooked 3-ounce serving: 205

STUFFING BASICS

If you enjoy the flavor of moist stuffing with your bird, you can bake the stuffing in a greased, covered casserole the last hour while your bird roasts. If you prefer stuffing your bird, follow these helpful hints:

• Only stuff chicken *immediately* before roasting. Stuffing poultry in advance can allow harmful bacteria to multiply and cause food poisoning.
• The cavity of the bird should be lightly stuffed because the stuffing expands as it cooks.
• Roasting a stuffed bird requires approximately three additional minutes of roasting time per pound of bird.
• Stuffing should come to an internal temperature of 165° for food safety reasons. It's wise to check the temperature of both the stuffing and meat in several places.
• After you've finished enjoying the bird and stuffing, separate the leftover meat from the stuffing and refrigerate immediately.

TIMETABLE FOR ROASTING

READY-TO-COOK WEIGHT	OVEN TEMPERATURE	APPROXIMATE TIME
BROILER-FRYER		
1½ to 2 pounds	400°F	¾ to 1 hour
2 to 2½ pounds	400°F	1 to 1¼ hours
2½ to 3 pounds	375°F	1¼ to 1¾ hours
3 to 4 pounds	375°F	1¾ to 2¼ hours
CAPON (Stuffed)		
5 to 8 pounds	325°F	2½ to 3½ hours

NOTE: Times given are for unstuffed chickens; stuffed birds require 15 to 30 minutes longer.

Bread Stuffing

¾ cup margarine or butter
1½ cups chopped celery (with leaves)
¾ cup finely chopped onion
9 cups soft bread cubes
1 teaspoon salt
½ teaspoon ground sage
1½ teaspoons chopped fresh or ½ teaspoon dried thyme leaves
¼ teaspoon pepper

Heat margarine in Dutch oven over medium-high heat. Cook celery and onion in margarine about 2 minutes. Remove from heat. Stir in remaining ingredients. **5 cups stuffing**

CASEROLE STUFFING: Place stuffing in un-greased 2-quart casserole. Cover and bake in 375° oven about 30 minutes or until hot.

CORN BREAD STUFFING: Substitute corn bread cubes for the soft bread cubes. **5 cups stuffing**

MUSHROOM STUFFING: Cook and stir 2 cups sliced mushrooms with the celery and onion. **5 cups stuffing**

Chicken Gravy

2 tablespoons drippings (fat and juices)
2 tablespoons all-purpose flour
1 cup chicken broth*
Salt and pepper, to taste

Place chicken on warm platter; keep warm while preparing gravy. Pour drippings from roasting pan or skillet into bowl, leaving brown particles in pan. Return 2 tablespoons drippings to pan.

*Vegetable cooking water, tomato or vegetable juice can be substituted for part of the broth.

(Measure accurately because too little fat will make gravy lumpy.)

Stir in flour. (Measure accurately so gravy will not be greasy.) Cook over low heat, stirring constantly, until mixture is smooth and bubbly. Remove from heat; stir in broth. Heat to boiling, stirring constantly. Boil and stir 1 minute. Stir in few drops bottled browning sauce, if desired. If thinner gravy is desired, stir in additional broth or other liquid. Sprinkle with salt and pepper.

Broiled Chicken

3- to 3½-pound broiler-fryer chicken, cut into quarters or pieces
2 tablespoons margarine or butter, melted

Fold wing tips across back side of chicken quarters. Set oven control to broil. Brush chicken with 1 tablespoon margarine. Place chicken, skin sides down, on rack in broiler. Place broiler pan so top of chicken is 7 to 9 inches from heat. Broil 30 minutes. Sprinkle with salt and pepper. Turn chicken and brush with 1 tablespoon margarine. Broil 15 to 25 minutes longer or until chicken is brown and juices run clear. **6 servings**

TO GRILL: Cover and grill chicken, bone sides down, 5 to 6 inches from medium coals 40 to 60 minutes, turning and brushing with margarine, until juices run clear.

BROILED LEMON CHICKEN: Do not brush with margarine or butter. Cut 1 lemon in half. Rub and squeeze lemon over chicken. Brush with 2 tablespoons margarine or butter, melted. Mix ½ teaspoon salt, ½ teaspoon paprika and ⅛ teaspoon pepper. Sprinkle over chicken. Broil as directed.

Poached Chicken

Use Poached Chicken in salads, casseroles and other recipes. Use this method when you don't need the broth.

2½- to 3-pound broiler fryer chicken, cut into pieces
¼ cup water
½ teaspoon salt

Remove any excess fat from chicken and place water in Dutch oven; sprinkle with salt. Heat to boiling; reduce heat. Cover and simmer until thickest pieces are done, 45 to 60 minutes. Remove chicken from Dutch oven; cool 10 minutes. Remove chicken from bones and skin. Cover and refrigerate up to 2 days.

3 to 4 cups cut-up cooked chicken

Microwaving Poultry

Arrange poultry pieces skin side up with thickest parts to outside edge in a dish large enough to hold pieces in single layer. Cover tightly and microwave as directed below until juices run clear. Cook all white meat *only* until meat thermometer registers 165°. All other poultry should be cooked to an internal temperature of 180°. Let stand about 5 minutes after cooking.

TYPE	AMOUNT	POWER LEVEL	TIME
Chicken			
Broiler-fryer chicken, cut up	3 to 3½ pounds	High	15 to 20 minutes, rotating dish ½ turn after 10 minutes
Chicken breast halves, with skin and bones	About 1¼ pounds (two)	High	8 to 10 minutes, rotating dish ½ turn after 4 minutes
Chicken breast halves, skinless boneless	About 1½ pounds (four)	High	8 to 10 minutes, rotating dish ½ turn after 4 minutes
Chicken drumsticks, thighs	2 pounds	High	16 to 19 minutes, rotating dish ½ turn after 10 minutes
Chicken wings	3 to 3½ pounds	High	12 to 15 minutes, rotating dish ½ turn after 6 minutes

Menus

WEEKEND LUNCH
Chicken Pocket Sandwiches (page 2)
Cut-up Vegetables
Pretzels
Chocolate Chip Cookies
Milk

COOL SUMMER DINNER
Curried Chicken Salad (page 6)
Sliced Tomatoes
Pita Bread
Frozen Yogurt
Iced Tea

WARMING WINTER MEAL
Chicken and Dumplings (page 31)
Tossed Green Salad with Blue Cheese Dressing
Bread Pudding
Tea and Coffee

HURRY-UP DINNER
Chicken Breasts in Lemon-Caper Sauce
(page 35)
Hot Egg Noodles
Steamed Broccoli
Cookies and Fresh Fruit

CHINESE MEAL
Walnut Chicken (page 42)
Hot Cooked Rice
Fortune Cookies
Tea

PICNIC FARE
Buttermilk Fried Chicken (page 64)
Cornbread
Three-Bean Salad
Peaches
Gingerbread Squares
Lemonade

COMPANY DINNER
Roast Chicken with Herbs (page 59)
Chicken Gravy (page ix)
Mushroom Stuffing (page ix)
Green Beans and Pearl Onions
Cherry Pie with Vanilla Ice Cream
Coffee and Tea

NO-FUSS FAMILY DINNER
Grilled Tarragon Chicken Bundles (page 70)
Boiled New Potatoes
Garlic Bread
Apple Crisp

Open-Face Pita Sandwiches

1

Sensational Salads and Sandwiches

Open-Face Pita Sandwiches

This hearty sandwich makes a great supper.

- ½ jar (8-ounce size) sun-
  dried tomatoes in oil,
  drained and 2 tablespoons
  oil reserved
- 4 small skinless boneless
  chicken breast halves
  (about 1 pound), cut into
  about ½-inch pieces
- ¼ teaspoon Italian seasoning
- 1 small onion, thinly sliced
- ¼ cup grated Parmesan
  cheese
- 2 whole wheat pita breads
  (6 inches in diameter)
- ½ cup shredded mozzarella
  cheese (2 ounces)

Heat oven to 375°. Heat reserved oil in 10-inch skillet over medium-high heat until hot. Sauté chicken, Italian seasoning and onion in oil about 4 minutes, stirring frequently, until chicken turns white. Cut tomatoes into ¼-inch strips. Stir tomatoes and Parmesan cheese into chicken mixture.

Split each pita bread in half around edge with knife to make 4 rounds. Divide chicken mixture evenly among rounds. Sprinkle with mozzarella cheese. Bake about 5 minutes or until cheese is melted. **4 servings**

PER SERVING: Calories 315; Protein 35 g; Carbohydrate 26 g; Fat 8 g; Cholesterol 75 mg; Sodium 520 mg

Club Sandwiches

A favorite for lunch or a light dinner.

- Mayonnaise or salad dressing
- 18 slices bread, toasted
- 12 lettuce leaves
- 6 slices cooked chicken
- 18 slices tomato (about 3 medium)
- 12 slices bacon, crisply fried
- Salt and pepper to taste

Spread mayonnaise over 1 side of each slice toast. Place 1 lettuce leaf and 1 slice chicken on each of 6 toast slices. Cover with second slice toast. Top with lettuce loaf, 3 slices tomato and 2 slices bacon. Sprinkle with salt and pepper. Cover with third slice toast; secure with wooden picks. To serve, cut diagonally into triangles. **6 servings**

PER SERVING: Calories 635; Protein 36 g; Carbohydrate 42 g; Fat 36 g; Cholesterol 100 mg; Sodium 800 mg

NOTE: Cheddar or Swiss cheese, salami, fully cooked smoked ham, hard-cooked eggs or green pepper rings can be added to sandwiches if desired.

Chicken Salad Filling

A versatile filling for your sandwiches—add lettuce and tomato, if you wish, and try pita bread, bagels or croissants for a different sandwich.

1½ cups chopped cooked chicken or turkey
½ cup mayonnaise or salad dressing
1 medium stalk celery, chopped (about ½ cup)
1 small onion, chopped (about ¼ cup)
¼ teaspoon salt
¼ teaspoon pepper

Mix all ingredients.   **4 servings**

PER SERVING: Calories 300; Protein 16 g; Carbohydrate 2 g; Fat 26 g; Cholesterol 45 mg; Sodium 345 mg

Extra-Special Chicken Salad

Chicken-salad sandwiches are classic, but when you want a little variety, try these tips for more zip in your chicken salad.

• Crumble bacon into your salad.
• Make the salad with a flavored mayonnaise, such as lemon or dill.
• Load up on extra vegetables such as tomatoes, cucumbers, sprouts, pea pods, zucchini, peppers, green onions and mushrooms, in your favorite combinations.
• Add a touch of horseradish to the mayonnaise for extra tang.
• Add capers, black olives, green olives or marinated artichoke hearts.
• Stir in walnuts for extra crunch.

Chicken Pocket Sandwiches

½ cup plain yogurt
1 tablespoon snipped chives or chopped onion
1 tablespoon lemon juice
1 teaspoon garlic salt
3 drops red pepper sauce
1½ cups cut-up cooked chicken
1 cup shredded natural Swiss, Monterey Jack or Cheddar cheese (about 4 ounces)
1 medium avocado, cut up
1 medium tomato, coarsely chopped
6 pita breads (6 inches in diameter)
1 cup alfalfa sprouts or shredded lettuce

Mix yogurt, chives, lemon juice, garlic salt and pepper sauce; toss with chicken, cheese, avocado and tomato. Cut or tear pita breads into halves. Split each pita bread halfway around edge with knife. Separate to form pocket. Alternate chicken mixture and alfalfa sprouts in pita bread halves, allowing about ¼ cup chicken mixture in each half.   **6 servings**

PER SERVING: Calories 400; Protein 34 g; Carbohydrate 30 g; Fat 16 g; Cholesterol 85 mg; Sodium 520 mg

Chicken Reuben Sandwiches

The traditional Reuben sandwich features corned beef—our version uses chicken for a great new taste.

¼ **cup Thousand Island dressing**
8 **slices rye or pumpernickel bread**
4 **slices natural Swiss cheese**
4 **slices cooked chicken**
1 **cup sauerkraut, drained**

Spread dressing over 4 slices bread; top with cheese, chicken and sauerkraut. Top with remaining slices bread. (If desired, spread margarine or butter over both sides of each sandwich.) Cook uncovered in skillet over low heat until bottoms are golden brown and cheese begins to melt, 5 to 7 minutes on each side.

4 servings

PER SERVING: Calories 465; Protein 38 g; Carbohydrate 31 g; Fat 21 g; Cholesterol 100 mg; Sodium 1000 mg

CHICKEN RACHEL SANDWICHES: Substitute 1 cup coleslaw for the sauerkraut.

Chicken Barbecue Sandwiches

½ **cup ketchup**
¼ **cup vinegar**
2 **tablespoons chopped onion**
1 **tablespoon Worcestershire sauce**
1 **teaspoon packed brown sugar**
¼ **teaspoon dry mustard**
1 **clove garlic, crushed**
1½ **cups cut-up cooked chicken**
4 **hamburger buns, split**

Heat all ingredients except chicken and buns to boiling over medium heat, stirring constantly; reduce heat. Simmer uncovered, stirring occasionally, 10 minutes; stir in chicken. Cover and simmer until chicken is hot, about 5 minutes. Fill hamburger buns with chicken mixture.

4 servings

PER SERVING: Calories 355; Protein 34 g; Carbohydrate 34 g; Fat 9 g; Cholesterol 90 mg; Sodium 690 mg

NOTE: 3 packages (3 ounces each) thinly sliced smoked chicken, cut into 1-inch strips, can be substituted for the 1½ cups cut-up chicken.

Chicken and Artichoke Croissants

4 **croissants, split lengthwise into halves**
1 **cup sliced mushrooms (about 3 ounces)**
3 **tablespoons margarine or butter**
1 **tablespoon all-purpose flour**
½ **teaspoon garlic salt**
½ **cup milk**
¼ **cup dry white wine or chicken broth**
1 **cup cut-up cooked chicken or turkey**
½ **cup shredded Swiss cheese (2 ounces)**
1 **jar (6 ounces) marinated artichoke hearts, drained and cut into halves**

Heat croissants in 300° oven until hot, about 10 minutes. Cook and stir mushrooms in 2 tablespoons of the margarine in 1½-quart saucepan over medium heat until tender, 2 to 3 minutes. Remove mushrooms; reserve.

Heat remaining 1 tablespoon margarine in same saucepan until melted; stir in the flour and garlic salt. Cook, stirring constantly, until bubbly. Remove from heat; stir in milk and wine. Heat to boiling, stirring constantly. Boil and stir 1 minute.

Stir in mushrooms and remaining ingredients; heat until hot. Spoon over croissant bottoms; add tops.

4 servings

PER SERVING: Calories 490; Protein 30 g; Carbohydrate 25 g; Fat 30 g; Cholesterol 105 mg; Sodium 740 mg

Chicken-filled Puffs

These elegant puffs make wonderful appetizers.

Mini Puffs (below)
2 cups finely chopped cooked chicken or
   3 cans (6¾ ounces each) chicken,
   drained
⅓ cup mayonnaise or salad dressing
1 tablespoon finely chopped onion or
   ½ teaspoon instant minced onion
1 teaspoon ground ginger
2 teaspoons lemon juice
½ teaspoon salt
¼ teaspoon pepper
2 stalks celery, finely chopped (about
   ½ cup)

Prepare Mini Puffs. Mix remaining ingredients. Cover and refrigerate no longer than 24 hours.

Cut off tops of puffs with sharp knife; remove any filaments of soft dough. Fill each puff with rounded teaspoon chicken mixture; replace top. Refrigerate until serving time.   **60 servings**

PER SERVING: Calories 45; Protein 3 g; Carbohydrate 2 g; Fat 3 g; Cholesterol 25 mg; Sodium 60 mg

Mini Puffs

1 cup water
½ cup margarine or butter
1 cup all-purpose flour
4 eggs

Heat oven to 400°. Heat water and margarine to rolling boil in 3-quart saucepan. Stir in flour. Stir vigorously over low heat until mixture forms a ball, about 1 minute; remove from heat. Beat in eggs, all at once; continue beating until smooth and glossy. Drop dough by slightly rounded teaspoonfuls onto ungreased cookie sheet. Bake until puffed, golden brown and dry, about 25 minutes. Cool on wire rack.

Chicken and Orange Salad

A cool salad for a warm day.

2 tablespoons finely chopped scallions
   or green onions (with tops)
2 tablespoons lime juice
¼ teaspoon salt
2 cups cut-up cooked chicken
1 cup cooked green peas
1 cup mayonnaise or salad dressing
¼ cup finely chopped carrot
¼ cup finely chopped celery
¼ cup finely snipped fresh cilantro
3 tablespoons orange juice
½ teaspoon salt
½ teaspoon ground cinnamon
¼ teaspoon freshly ground pepper
Lettuce leaves
3 oranges, pared and sectioned or unpared and cut into wedges
2 avocados, peeled and cut into wedges

Sprinkle scallions with lime juice and ¼ teaspoon salt; cover and refrigerate. Mix remaining ingredients except lettuce, oranges and avocados; cover and refrigerate at least 1 hour.

Spoon chicken mixture onto lettuce. Garnish with oranges and avocados; sprinkle with scallions.   **6 servings**

PER SERVING: Calories 680; Protein 32 g; Carbohydrate 23 g; Fat 55 g; Cholesterol 100 mg; Sodium 590 mg

Chicken and Orange Salad

Chicken Salad with Honey Dressing

Honey Dressing (below)
3 cups cut-up cooked chicken
1½ cups seedless grapes
¼ cup sliced green onions (with tops)
¼ cup chopped green bell pepper
1 can (8 ounces) water chestnuts,
   drained and chopped
2 oranges, pared and sectioned
¼ head lettuce, torn into bite-size pieces
   (about 3 cups)
¼ cup toasted slivered almonds

Prepare Honey Dressing. Toss with chicken, grapes, onions, bell pepper and water chestnuts. Cover and refrigerate until chilled, at least 2 hours.

Toss chicken mixture with orange sections and lettuce. Spoon onto salad greens, if desired; sprinkle with almonds.   **6 servings**

PER SERVING: Calories 460; Protein 43 g; Carbohydrate 23 g; Fat 22 g; Cholesterol 115 mg; Sodium 440 mg

Honey Dressing

¼ cup vegetable oil
2 tablespoons vinegar
1 tablespoon honey
¾ teaspoon salt
Dash of pepper
4 to 6 drops red pepper sauce

Shake all ingredients in tightly covered container.

Curried Chicken Salad

3 cups cold cooked rice
2 cups cut-up cooked chicken or turkey
2 medium stalks celery, sliced (about 1
   cup)
1 small green bell pepper, chopped
   (about ½ cup)
1 can (13¼ ounces) pineapple chunks,
   drained
1 cup mayonnaise or salad dressing
¾ teaspoon curry powder
¼ teaspoon salt
¼ teaspoon ground ginger
Salad greens
2 medium tomatoes, cut into wedges
6 slices bacon, crisply cooked and
   crumbled

Mix rice, chicken, celery, bell pepper and pineapple. Mix mayonnaise, curry powder, salt and ginger. Stir into chicken mixture. Cover and refrigerate about 2 hours or until chilled.

Just before serving, spoon chicken mixture onto salad greens. Garnish with tomato wedges and sprinkle with bacon.   **6 servings**

PER SERVING: Calories 555; Protein 17 g; Carbohydrate 37 g; Fat 38 g; Cholesterol 45 mg; Sodium 785 mg

Cobb Salads

Lemon Vinaigrette (below)
6 cups finely shredded lettuce
2 cups cut-up cooked chicken
3 hard-cooked eggs, chopped
2 medium tomatoes, chopped (about
   1½ cups)
1 ripe avocado, chopped
¼ cup crumbled blue cheese (1 ounce)
4 slices bacon, crisply cooked and
   crumbled

Prepare Lemon Vinaigrette. Divide lettuce among 4 salad plates or bowls. Arrange remaining ingredients in rows on lettuce. Serve with Lemon Vinaigrette. **4 servings**

PER SERVING: Calories 650; Protein 29 g; Carbohydrate 13 g; Fat 55 g; Cholesterol 275 mg; Sodium 555 mg

Lemon Vinaigrette

½ cup vegetable oil
¼ cup lemon juice
1 tablespoon red wine vinegar
2 teaspoons sugar
½ teaspoon salt
½ teapsoon dry mustard
½ teaspoon Worcestershire sauce
¼ teaspoon garlic powder
¼ teaspoon pepper

Shake all ingredients in tightly covered container. Refrigerate at least 1 hour.

Chicken, Spinach and Tomato Salad

¼ cup olive oil
1 small onion, chopped (about ¼ cup)
6 skinless boneless chicken breast
   halves (about 1½ pounds)
½ cup dry white wine or chicken broth
½ cup olive oil
2 tablespoons lemon juice
2 tablespoons chopped fresh rosemary
2 tablespoons chopped fresh basil
2 tablespoons chopped fresh mint
½ teaspoon salt
¼ teaspoon pepper
1 pound fresh spinach leaves
6 medium tomatoes, sliced
¼ cup freshly grated Parmesan cheese

Heat ¼ cup oil in 12-inch skillet over medium-high heat. Sauté onion in oil. Reduce heat to medium; add chicken breasts. Cook uncovered about 5 minutes, turning frequently, until chicken is brown; add wine. Cover and simmer about 10 minutes or until chicken is done. Cover and refrigerate until cold.

Cut chicken into strips. Mix ½ cup oil, the lemon juice, rosemary, basil, mint, salt and pepper. Arrange one-third of the spinach on large platter; top with one-third of the tomatoes and one-third of the chicken. Repeat twice with remaining spinach, tomatoes and chicken; drizzle with oil mixture. Sprinkle with cheese. Garnish with fresh rosemary, basil or mint leaves if desired. **6 servings**

PER SERVING: Calories 445; Protein 29 g; Carbohydrate 10 g; Fat 32 g; Cholesterol 65 mg; Sodium 370 mg

Chicken-Papaya Salad

4 cups water
2 whole chicken breasts (about 2
   pounds)
Gingered Pineapple Dressing (below)
4 ounces Chinese pea pods
1 large papaya
1 small green onion (with top), chopped
Lettuce leaves

Heat water to boiling; add chicken. Heat to boiling; reduce heat to medium. Cover and simmer 10 minutes; remove from heat. Let stand covered 15 minutes; remove chicken from broth. Cool slightly; remove bones and skin from chicken. Cover and refrigerate chicken until cold.

Cut chicken into 1-inch pieces. Prepare Gingered Pineapple Dressing. Toss chicken and half of the dressing. Let stand 10 minutes.

Remove strings from pea pods. Place pea pods in boiling water; heat to boiling. Immediately rinse in cold water; drain. Cut pea pods into halves. Pare papaya; cut into ³/₄-inch pieces. Toss chicken mixture, pea pods, papaya, green onion and remaining dressing until evenly coated. Arrange lettuce leaves on serving platter. Spoon chicken mixture on lettuce; garnish with diced pimiento or red bell pepper if desired.   **4 servings**

PER SERVING: Calories 495; Protein 35 g; Carbohydrate 28 g; Fat 27 g; Cholesterol 100 mg; Sodium 240 mg

Gingered Pineapple Dressing

¹/₂ cup mayonnaise or salad dressing
¹/₄ cup pineapple preserves
2 tablespoons lemon juice
1 teaspoon sugar
1 teaspoon gingerroot juice
1 teaspoon sesame oil

Mix all ingredients.

NOTE: To make gingerroot juice, press thin slices of fresh gingerroot in a garlic press, or squeeze finely chopped gingerroot between your fingers to extract the juice.

Chicken-Pasta Salad

1 package (6 ounces)
   frozen pea pods
1 package (5 ounces) spiral
   macaroni
¹/₃ cup mayonnaise or salad
   dressing
¹/₄ cup French dressing
2 cups cut-up cooked chicken
   (about 12 ounces)
1 cup cherry tomatoes, cut
   into halves

Remove pea pods from package. Place pea pods in bowl of cool water until thawed; drain. Cook macaroni as directed on package—except add pea pods about 2 minutes before macaroni is done; drain. Rinse macaroni and pea pods with cold water; drain. Mix mayonnaise and French dressing in large bowl. Add macaroni mixture and remaining ingredients; toss.

4 servings

PER SERVING: Calories 605; Protein 48 g; Carbohydrate 36 g; Fat 30 g; Cholesterol 135 mg; Sodium 430 mg

Chicken-Pasta Salad

Green Tortellini-Chicken Salad

Starting with tortellini from the refrigerated food section of your grocery store makes preparing this salad extra easy.

1 cup parsley sprigs
⅓ cup grated Parmesan cheese
1½ cups large curd creamed
   cottage cheese
1 tablespoon lemon juice
1 tablespoon milk
½ teaspoon dried basil leaves
½ teaspoon salt
⅛ teaspoon pepper
4 to 6 drops red pepper sauce
2 cloves garlic, crushed
1 package (9 ounces) fresh
   cheese-filled tortellini
1 cup cut-up cooked chicken

Place all ingredients except tortellini and chicken in blender. Cover and blend on high speed about 3 minutes, stopping blender occasionally to scrape sides, until smooth. Cover and refrigerate at least 2 hours but no longer than 24 hours.

Cook the tortellini as directed on package; drain. Toss with green sauce and chicken.

4 servings

PER SERVING: Calories 435; Protein 32 g; Carbohydrate 51 g; Fat 11 g; Cholesterol 110 mg; Sodium 780 mg

Cutting Calories in Salads

Chicken salad is an excellent choice for calorie counters, especially when you use a low-calorie dressing. Follow these tips to shape up your chicken salads.

• Use as little oil as possible, substituting highly flavored ingredients such as flavored vinegars, unsweetened fruit juices, lemon or lime juice. See Wilted Chicken Salad (page 14) and Waldorf Chicken (page 16) as examples of how to pare down calories while keeping great flavor.

• Avoid creamy dressings, which tend to be high in fat, or buy reduced-fat versions of these dressings.

• Use nonfat yogurt in place of mayonnaise, or use a half-mayonnaise, half-yogurt mixture to save on calories.

• Make your own vinaigrette salad dressing. Most recipes call for 3 parts oil to 1 part vinegar. Try using 1 part oil to 1 part of a mild vinegar, such as balsamic or raspberry.

Oriental Chicken Salad

Cellophane noodles are hard, clear noodles made from mung peas. They become white, puffy and crisp when deep-fried, puffing up to more than twice their original size. Remove them quickly from the oil so they stay white.

Ginger Dressing (right)
Vegetable oil
1 package (3¾ ounces) cellophane noodles (bean threads)*
½ head lettuce, shredded (about 4 cups)
3 cups cut-up cooked chicken or turkey
1 medium carrot, shredded (about ½ cup)
4 green onions (with tops) sliced (about ¼ cup)
1 tablespoon sesame seed, toasted

Prepare Ginger Dressing. Heat oil (1 inch) in Dutch oven to 425°. Fry ¼ of the noodles at a time about 5 seconds, turning once, until puffed; drain.

Pour Ginger Dressing over lettuce, chicken, carrot and onions in large bowl. Toss with half of the noodles. Place remaining noodles on large platter. Spoon salad over noodles. Sprinkle with sesame seed.   **6 servings**

PER SERVING: Calories 490; Protein 25 g; Carbohydrate 28 g; Fat 31 g; Cholesterol 65 mg; Sodium 650 mg

Ginger Dressing

⅓ cup vegetable oil
¼ cup white wine vinegar
1 tablespoon sugar
2 teaspoons soy sauce
½ teaspoon pepper
½ teaspoon ground ginger
¼ teaspoon salt

Shake all ingredients in tightly covered container. Refrigerate at least 2 hours.

Colorful Pasta Salad

½ package (16-ounce size) rigatoni or ziti macaroni
2 cups cut-up cooked chicken
2 medium tomatoes, chopped (about 2 cups)
2 green onions (with tops), sliced
2 cloves garlic, crushed
3 tablespoons chopped fresh parsley
1½ teaspoons chopped fresh or ½ teaspoon dried basil leaves
¼ teaspoon salt
¼ teaspoon coarsely cracked pepper
2 tablespoons olive or vegetable oil

Cook rigatoni as directed on package; drain. Mix remaining ingredients. Toss with rigatoni. Cover and refrigerate at least 2 hours but no longer than 24 hours. Toss before serving. Serve with freshly ground pepper if desired.

6 servings

PER SERVING: Calories 275; Protein 18 g; Carbohydrate 31 g; Fat 8 g; Cholesterol 40 mg; Sodium 130 mg

5 cups chow mein noodles can be substituted for the fried cellophane noodles. Toss half of the noodles with chicken-dressing mixture. Continue as directed.

Hot German Chicken Salad

A great quick dinner on a chilly day!

- 4 skinless boneless chicken breast halves (about 1 pound)
- 2 tablespoons vegetable oil
- 1 tablespoon all-purpose flour
- 1/4 teaspoon salt
- 1/8 teaspoon pepper
- 1/2 cup water
- 2 tablespoons white wine vinegar
- 2 teaspoons Dijon mustard
- 2 teaspoons chopped fresh or 1/2 teaspoon dried thyme
- 2 ounces mushrooms, sliced (about 3/4 cup)
- 2 green onions (with tops), thinly sliced
- 1/2 bunch romaine, torn into bite-size pieces
- 2 medium tomatoes, cut into wedges

Cook chicken breast halves in oil in 10-inch non-stick skillet over medium heat about 6 minutes on each side or until done. Remove chicken from skillet; drain. Cool chicken slightly and cut into thin slices.

Stir flour, salt and pepper into drippings in skillet. Cook over low heat, stirring constantly, until smooth and bubbly; remove from heat. Stir in water, vinegar, mustard, thyme, mushrooms and green onions. Cook over low heat, stirring constantly, until mixture is bubbly. Cook and stir 1 minute. Divide romaine among 4 salad plates. Arrange chicken and tomatoes on romaine. Spoon mushroom mixture over top.

4 servings

PER SERVING: Calories 225; Protein 27 g; Carbohydrate 7 g; Fat 10 g; Cholesterol 60 mg; Sodium 230 mg

Thai Chicken Salad

After handling the chili, wash your hands thoroughly with soap and water to remove every trace of its oil.

- 4 small dried cloud ears or 2 pieces dried black fungus
- 1/2 package (3 3/4 ounces) cellophane noodles, (bean threads)
- 2 green onions (with tops), thinly sliced
- 1 small whole chicken breast, cooked, skinned and shredded
- 4 ounces medium shrimp (about 6), cooked and coarsely chopped
- 1/2 cup shredded fresh spinach
- 1/4 cup coarsely chopped peanuts
- 1 tablespoon snipped mint leaves
- Romaine or leaf lettuce leaves
- Snipped fresh cilantro
- Dressing (below)

Cover cloud ears with hot water. Let stand 20 minutes; drain. Cut into thin slices. Cover cellophane noodles with cold water. Let stand 10 minutes; drain. Cook noodles in boiling water until tender, about 10 minutes; drain. Cut noodles to shorten strands; cool.

Mix green onions, chicken, shrimp, spinach, peanuts and mint. Line a small platter with romaine leaves; arrange cellophane noodles on top. Spoon chicken mixture over noodles. Sprinkle with cilantro and cloud ears. Serve with Dressing.

4 servings

PER SERVING: Calories 240; Protein 23 g; Carbohydrate 23 g; Fat 6 g; Cholesterol 85 mg; Sodium 650 mg

Dressing:

- 1/4 cup lemon juice
- 3 tablespoons fish sauce
- 2 teaspoons sugar
- 1 serrano chili, seeded and chopped

Mix all ingredients.

Thai Chicken Salad

Wilted Spinach and Chicken Salad

1 skinless boneless whole chicken
  breast (about ½ pound)
4 slices bacon
1 tablespoon sesame seed
¼ cup vinegar
2 teaspoons sugar
1 teaspoon cornstarch
½ teaspoon salt
¼ teaspoon pepper
1 pound spinach
½ small red onion, thinly sliced

Cut chicken breast into 1-inch pieces; reserve. Cook bacon in Dutch oven over medium heat until crisp. Drain bacon, reserving fat in Dutch oven. Crumble bacon. Stir chicken and sesame seed into fat in Dutch oven. Cook over medium heat 6 to 7 minutes, stirring occasionally, until chicken is white.

Mix vinegar, sugar, cornstarch, salt and pepper. Stir into chicken mixture. Heat to boiling, stirring constantly. Boil and stir 1 minute; remove from heat. Add spinach and onion. Toss 2 to 3 minutes or until spinach is wilted. Sprinkle with bacon. Serve immediately.   **4 servings**

PER SERVING: Calories 295; Protein 16 g; Carbohydrate 10 g; Fat 22 g; Cholesterol 60 mg; Sodium 460 mg

Hot Chicken Salad with Plum Sauce

2 teaspoons olive or vegetable oil
4 skinless boneless chicken breast
  halves (about 1 pound)
1 can (16 ounces) purple plums in juice,
  rinsed, drained and pitted
1 tablespoon lemon juice
2 teaspoons packed brown sugar
¼ teaspoon ground ginger
⅛ teaspoon crushed red pepper
1 clove garlic
4 cups shredded Chinese cabbage
1 cup bean sprouts (about 2 ounces)
1 tablespoon thinly sliced green onion
  with top (about ½ medium)

Heat oil in 10-inch nonstick skillet over medium heat. Cook chicken breast halves, turning once, about 10 minutes or until done.

Place remaining ingredients except cabbage, bean sprouts and onion in blender or food processor. Cover and blend on high speed or process about 30 seconds or until smooth. Heat sauce if desired.

Arrange cabbage, bean sprouts and onion on 4 serving plates. Top with chicken. Spoon plum sauce over chicken.   **4 servings**

PER SERVING: Calories 220; Protein 28 g; Carbohydrate 16 g; Fat 4 g; Cholesterol 65 mg; Sodium 140 mg

Hot Chicken Salad with Plum Sauce

Waldorf Chicken

This is an unusual variation on the popular salad that turns chicken into a masterpiece.

6 small chicken breast halves (about 3 pounds), skinned and boned
1 cup unsweetened apple juice
1 tablespoon lemon juice
¼ teaspooon salt
¼ teaspoon ground ginger
1 tablespoon cornstarch
2 cups coarsely chopped unpared red apples (about 2 medium)
1 cup diagonally cut celery slices (about 2 medium stalks)
3 tablespoons raisins
1 tablespoon sliced green onion (with top)

Remove fat from chicken. Place chicken, ½ cup of the apple juice, the lemon juice, salt and ginger in 10-inch nonstick skillet. Heat to boiling; reduce heat. Cover and simmer until done, about 20 minutes. Remove chicken; keep warm.

Mix remaining apple juice and the cornstarch; add to hot liquid. Heat to boiling, stirring constantly. Boil and stir 1 minute. Stir in remaining ingredients; heat through. For each serving, diagonally slice chicken breast, overlapping slices. Top with sauce. **6 servings**

PER SERVING: Calories 240; Protein 33 g; Carbohydrate 18 g; Fat 4 g; Cholesterol 85 mg; Sodium 180 mg

MICROWAVE DIRECTIONS: Decrease apple juice to ¾ cup. Place chicken, ½ cup of the apple juice, the lemon juice, salt and ginger in 3-quart microwavable casserole. Cover tightly and microwave on high 6 minutes; rotate casserole ½ turn. Microwave until chicken is done, 6 to 8 minutes longer. Remove chicken; keep warm. Mix remaining apple juice and the cornstarch; add to hot liquid. Microwave uncovered, stirring every minute until thickened, 3 to 4 minutes. Stir in remaining ingredients and microwave until hot, 2 to 3 minutes. Continue as directed.

Waldorf Chicken

2

Savory Soups and Stews

═══════════════◧═══════════════

Chicken and Broth

Making your own broth is a wonderful way to start a soup.

3- to 3½-pound broiler-fryer chicken, cut
   up*
4½ cups cold water
1 teaspoon salt
½ teaspoon pepper
1 stalk celery with leaves, cut up
1 medium carrot, cut up
1 small onion, cut up
1 sprig parsley

Remove any excess fat from chicken. Place chicken, giblets (except liver) and neck in Dutch oven. Add remaining ingredients and heat to boiling. Skim foam from broth; reduce heat. Cover and simmer about 45 minutes or until juices of chicken run clear.

Remove chicken from broth. Cool chicken about 10 minutes or just until cool enough to handle. Strain broth through cheesecloth-lined sieve; discard vegetables. Remove skin and bones from chicken. Cut up chicken. Skim fat from

3 to 3½ pounds chicken necks, backs and giblets (except liver) can be used to make broth.

broth. Cover and refrigerate broth and chicken in separate containers no longer than 24 hours, or freeze for future use. **About 3 cups cooked chicken; about 3 cups broth**

PER SERVING (CHICKEN): Calories 335; Protein 38 g; Carbohydrate 0 g; Fat 19 g; Cholesterol 125 mg; Sodium 115 mg
PER SERVING (BROTH): Calories 40; Protein 5 g; Carbohydrate 1 g; Fat 1 g; Cholesterol 0 mg; Sodium 775 mg

Saving Chicken Parts for Soup

When you cut up a chicken, save the necks, backs and giblets (except the livers) to make chicken broth or soup. Keep two heavy plastic bags in your freezer— one for accumulating necks, backs and giblets, and the other for chicken livers. Cook the necks, backs and giblets to make Chicken and Broth (left) or Chicken-Noodle Soup (page 19). When you have saved enough livers for a meal, make Creamed Chicken Livers on Toast (page 58) or your favorite liver dish.

Chicken-Noodle Soup

Chicken and Broth
2 medium carrots, sliced (about 1 cup)
2 medium stalks celery, sliced (about 1
cup)
1 small onion, chopped (about ¼ cup)
1 tablespoon instant chicken bouillon
1 cup uncooked medium noodles (about
2 ounces)

Prepare Chicken and Broth. Reserve cut-up chicken. Add enough water to broth to measure 5 cups. Heat broth, carrots, celery, onion and bouillon (dry) to boiling; reduce heat. Cover and simmer about 15 minutes or until carrots are tender. Stir in noodles and chicken. Heat to boiling; reduce heat. Simmer uncovered 7 to 10 minutes or until noodles are tender. Sprinkle with chopped parsley if desired. **6 servings**

PER SERVING: Calories 295; Protein 31 g; Carbohydrate 7 g; Fat 15 g; Cholesterol 90 mg; Sodium 670 mg

CHICKEN-RICE SOUP: Substitute ½ cup uncooked regular long grain rice for the uncooked noodles. Stir in rice with the vegetables. Cover and simmer about 15 minutes or until rice is tender. Stir in chicken and heat until chicken is hot.

Chicken and Leek Soup

This chicken soup is enhanced with the flavor of leeks, the national symbol of Wales, though the soup is of Scottish origin.

2½ pound broiler-fryer chicken,
cut up
4 cups water
1 medium carrot, sliced
1 medium stalk celery, sliced*
½ cup barley
2 teaspoons instant chicken bouillon
2 teaspoons salt
¼ teaspoon pepper
1 bay leaf
1½ cups sliced leeks (with tops)

Heat all ingredients except leeks to boiling in Dutch oven; reduce heat. Cover and simmer 30 minutes. Add leeks. Heat to boiling; reduce heat. Cover and simmer until thickest pieces of chicken are done, about 15 minutes. Remove chicken from broth; cool slightly. Remove chicken from bones and skin; cut chicken into 1-inch pieces. Skim fat from broth; remove bay leaf. Add chicken to broth; heat until hot, about 5 minutes.

7 servings (about 1 cup each)

PER SERVING: Calories 245; Protein 32 g; Carbohydrate 14 g; Fat 7 g; Cholesterol 85 mg; Sodium 710 mg

1 package (10 ounces) frozen mixed vegetables (about 2 cups) can be substituted for the carrots and celery.

Chicken-Cabbage Soup

If you are concerned about sodium and would like to lower your sodium consumption, use low-sodium eight-vegetable juice and bouillon granules.

5 cups finely chopped cabbage (about 1¼ pounds)
3 cups eight-vegetable juice
2 cups water
2 cups ¼-inch slices carrots (about 4 medium)
1 cup chopped celery (about 2 medium stalks)
1 medium onion, sliced
2 tablespoons instant chicken bouillon
¼ teaspoon pepper
3- to 3½-pound broiler-fryer chicken, cut up
½ teaspoon paprika
2 tablespoons reduced-calorie margarine

Heat cabbage, vegetable juice, water, carrots, celery, onion, bouillon (dry) and pepper to boiling in 4-quart Dutch oven; reduce heat. Cover and simmer 30 minutes.

Remove skin and any excess fat from chicken pieces. Cut each breast half into halves. Sprinkle chicken with paprika. Heat margarine in 10-inch nonstick skillet. Cook chicken 15 to 20 minutes or until light brown on all sides. Add chicken to soup mixture. Heat to boiling; reduce heat. Cover and simmer about 30 minutes or until juices of thickest chicken pieces run clear. Serve chicken pieces in soup bowls; pour soup over chicken. **6 servings**

PER SERVING: Calories 315; Protein 39 g; Carbohydrate 17 g; Fat 10 g; Cholesterol 110 mg; Sodium 850 mg

Chicken-Vegetable Soup

The chicken is skinned for a low-fat broth. To lower sodium, use low-sodium bouillon.

3 cups tomato-vegetable juice
2 cups water
5 cups finely chopped cabbage
1 medium onion sliced
2 cups ¼-inch carrot slices (about 4 medium)
1 cup chopped celery (about 2 medium stalks)
2 tablespoons chicken bouillon granules
¼ teaspoon pepper
3-pound broiler-fryer chicken, cut up and skinned
½ teaspoon salt
½ teaspoon paprika
2 tablespoons reduced-calorie margarine

Heat tomato-vegetable juice, water, cabbage, onion, carrots, celery, bouillon (dry) and pepper to boiling in 4-quart nonstick Dutch oven; reduce heat. Cover and simmer 30 minutes.

Remove excess fat from chicken; cut each chicken breast half into halves; sprinkle chicken with salt and paprika. Heat margarine in 10-inch skillet over medium heat until hot. Cook chicken in margarine until light brown on all sides, 15 to 20 minutes. Add chicken to soup. Heat to boiling; reduce heat.

Cover and simmer until chicken is done, about 30 minutes longer. Place chicken in soup bowls; pour soup over chicken. **8 servings**

PER SERVING: Calories 170; Protein 19 g; Carbohydrate 13 g; Fat 5 g; Cholesterol 45 mg; Sodium 1010 mg

Chicken-Vegetable Soup

Chicken-Rice Soup with Vegetables

2½ to 3 pounds chicken backs, necks
   and/or wings
5 cups water
1½ teaspoons salt
1 teaspoon instant chicken bouillon
1 teaspoon chili powder
¼ teaspoon pepper
1 bay leaf
2 medium carrots, sliced (about 1 cup)
2 medium stalks celery, sliced (about 1
   cup)*
1 small onion, chopped (about ¼ cup)
1 can (15½ ounces) kidney
   beans, undrained
¼ cup uncooked regular rice
Snipped parsley

Heat chicken, water, salt, bouillon (dry), chili powder, pepper and bay leaf to boiling in Dutch oven; reduce heat. Cover and simmer until chicken is done, 45 to 60 minutes.

Remove chicken from broth; cool chicken 10 minutes. Remove chicken from bones and skin. Skim fat from broth; strain broth. Add enough water to broth, if necessary, to measure 5 cups. Heat broth and remaining ingredients except parsley to boiling; reduce heat. Cover and simmer until rice is tender, about 15 minutes. Stir in chicken; heat until hot. Sprinkle with parlsey.

5 servings (about 1½ cups each)

PER SERVING: Calories 270; Protein 21 g; Carbohydrate 29 g; Fat 8 g; Cholesterol 45 mg; Sodium 890 mg

Chicken and Bean Soup with Parsley

8 cups water
1 cup dried great northern beans
1 cup dried kidney beans
1 teaspoon rubbed sage
1 package (2.5 ounces) onion soup mix
   (2 envelopes)
2 whole skinless boneless chicken breasts,
   cut into 1-inch pieces (about 1 pound)
½ cup snipped parsley

Heat water, beans, sage and soup mix (dry) to boiling in 4-quart Dutch oven. Boil 2 minutes; reduce heat. Cover and simmer until beans are tender, about 2½ hours.

Stir in chicken and parsley. Cover and cook until chicken is done, about 15 minutes.

8 servings

PER SERVING: Calories 250; Protein 24 g; Carbohydrate 32 g; Fat 3 g; Cholesterol 30 mg; Sodium 830 mg

---

*1 package (10 ounces) frozen mixed vegetables (about 2 cups) can be substituted for the carrots and celery.

Chicken and Bean Soup with Parsley

Chicken and Barley Soup

2½- to 3-pound broiler-fryer chicken, cut
up, or 2½ pounds chicken pieces
6 cups water
1 large onion, coarsely chopped (about 1
cup)
½ cup uncooked regular barley
2 teaspoons instant chicken
bouillon
2 teaspoons salt
½ teaspoon dried marjoram
leaves
½ teaspoon dried thyme leaves
¼ teaspoon pepper
3 medium carrots, cut into
½-inch slices
1 medium turnip or rutabaga,
cut into ¾-inch pieces
1 clove garlic, finely chopped
1 bay leaf
2 medium stalks celery, cut
into ½-inch slices
1 cup frozen green peas

Remove any excess fat from chicken. Place
chicken and remaining ingredients except celery
and peas in 4-quart Dutch oven. Heat to boiling;
reduce heat. Cover and simmer until thickest
pieces of chicken are done, about 45 minutes.

Remove chicken from broth; skim fat from broth.
Stir celery into broth. Cover and heat to boiling;
reduce heat. Simmer until barley is tender, about
15 minutes. Remove chicken from bones and
skin; cut chicken into 1-inch pieces. Add chicken
and peas to soup; heat until hot, about 10
minutes.   **8 servings**

PER SERVING: Calories 240; Protein 29 g; Carbohydrate 18 g; Fat 6 g; Cholesterol 75 mg; Sodium 650 mg

Soup Shortcuts

You don't always have time to whip up your
own chicken broth. Canned soups and
broths are certainly delicious and convenient substitutes. Here are other ways to
cut down on preparation time without cutting down on flavor.

• To make broth from bouillon: For each
cup of broth, simply dissolve 1 bouillon
cube or 1 teaspoon instant bouillon in 1
cup of boiling water.

• Make an impromptu soup by adding leftover cooked vegetables and chicken to
broth or bouillon. Add your favorite spices
and some croutons or crackers for garnish,
and you have a delicious soup in no time.

• Salad bars in delis and groceries can be
a boon to the chef in a hurry. If you don't
have time to chop and peel vegetables for
soup, you can pick up already prepared
vegetables in many stores.

French-style Chicken Soup

2½- to 3-pound broiler-fryer chicken, cut up
2 tablespoons vegetable oil
2 large onions, thinly sliced and separated into rings
2 cloves garlic, finely chopped
1 cup water
1 cup dry white wine or apple juice
1 tablespoon sugar
1 teaspoon salt
1 teaspoon dried thyme leaves
¼ teaspoon pepper
1 can (16 ounces) whole tomatoes, undrained
1 can (10¾ ounces) condensed chicken broth
1 medium green bell pepper, cut into ¼-inch strips
8 slices French bread, toasted
Snipped parsley

Remove skin and any excess fat from chicken pieces. Heat oil in Dutch oven. Cook chicken in oil until brown on all sides; remove chicken from pan. Cook and stir onions and garlic in same pan until onions are tender. Return chicken to pan; add water, wine, sugar, salt, thyme, pepper, tomatoes and broth; break up tomatoes. Heat to boiling; reduce heat. Cover and simmer until chicken is done, about 1 hour.

Skim fat from chicken mixture. Add bell pepper. Heat to boiling; reduce heat. Cover and simmer just until bell pepper is tender, about 10 minutes. Place a slice of French bread in each serving bowl. Spoon chicken and broth over bread. Sprinkle with parsley.   **8 servings**

PER SERVING: Calories 320; Protein 34 g; Carbohydrate 23 g; Fat 10 g; Cholesterol 85 mg; Sodium 710 mg

Chicken Tortilla Soup

Based on the traditional Mexican soup sopa azteca, *this rich broth features crisp-fried tortilla strips and creamy slices of avocado.*

1 medium onion, finely chopped (about ½ cup)
1 clove garlic, finely chopped
2 tablespoons vegetable oil
4 cups chicken broth
¼ cup chopped red bell pepper
1 teaspoon ground red chilies
¾ teaspoon dried basil leaves
½ teaspoon salt
¼ teaspoon pepper
1 can (15 ounces) tomato puree
½ cup vegetable oil
10 corn tortillas (6 inches in diamater), cut into ½-inch strips
2 cups cut-up cooked chicken breasts
Shredded Monterey Jack or Chihuahua cheese
Avocado slices

Cook and stir onion and garlic in 2 tablespoons oil in 4-quart Dutch oven until onion is tender. Stir in broth, bell pepper, ground red chilies, basil, salt, pepper and tomato puree. Heat to boiling; reduce heat. Simmer uncovered 30 minutes.

Heat ½ cup oil in 10-inch skillet until hot. Cook tortilla strips in oil until light golden brown, 30 to 60 seconds; drain. Divide tortilla strips and chicken among 6 bowls; pour broth over chicken. Top with cheese and avocado slices.

6 servings

PER SERVING: Calories 570; Protein 39 g; Carbohydrate 39 g; Fat 35 g; Cholesterol 85 mg; Sodium 1200 mg

Chicken-Tortellini Soup

¼ cup margarine or butter
½ cup finely chopped onion (about 1 medium)
½ cup finely chopped celery (about 1 medium stalk)
4 skinless boneless chicken breast halves, cut into 1-inch pieces (about 1½ pounds)
¼ cup all-purpose flour
½ teaspoon pepper
4½ cups chicken broth
1 package (16 ounces) cheese-filled tortellini, cooked
Parmesan cheese

Heat margarine in large saucepan until melted. Cook and stir onion, celery and chicken in margarine over medium heat about 8 minutes or until chicken is done. Stir in flour and pepper; gradually add chicken broth. Cook over medium heat, stirring constantly, until mixture boils; boil 1 minute. Stir in tortellini; heat until warm. Serve with Parmesan cheese.   **8 servings**

PER SERVING: Calories 490; Protein 46 g; Carbohydrate 25 g; Fat 23 g; Cholesterol 185 mg; Sodium 1180 mg

Southwest Chicken Soup

You can substitute marinated or pickled red peppers for the fresh. They are available in many supermarkets in the refrigerated or shelf-stable sections. Be sure to drain the light brine in which they are packaged before using.

2 large red bell peppers
4 skinless boneless chicken breast halves (about 1 pound)
½ cup chopped onion (about 1 medium)
3 cups chicken broth
2 tablespoons lime juice
1 tablespoon chopped fresh cilantro
½ teaspoon salt
¼ teaspoon pepper
2 cloves garlic, crushed
2 cups cubed jicama

Set oven control to broil. Place bell peppers on rack in broiler pan. Broil with tops about 5 inches from heat, turning occasionally, until skin is blistered and evenly browned (not burned). Remove peppers to brown paper bag and close tightly. Let stand 20 minutes.

Place chicken beasts on rack in broiler pan. Broil with tops 5 to 7 inches from heat about 15 minutes, turning once, until juices of chicken run clear. Cool 10 minutes. Cut into bite-size pieces.

Pare peppers; discard skin. Place peppers and onion in blender or food processor. Cover and blend or process until smooth.

Heat pepper mixture, broth, lime juice, cilantro, salt, pepper and garlic to boiling in 2-quart saucepan; reduce heat. Simmer uncovered 15 minutes, stirring occasionally. Stir in chicken and jicama. Heat until hot.   **4 servings**

PER SERVING: Calories 215; Protein 33 g; Carbohydrate 13 g; Fat 3 g; Cholesterol 70 mg; Sodium 980 mg

Southwest Chicken Soup

Dumpling Soup

2 tablespoons olive oil
2 cloves garlic, finely chopped
1 medium onion, thinly sliced
1 pound chicken livers, cut up
4 cups chicken broth
2 cups water
1/2 cup dry white wine or chicken broth
1/2 cup snipped fresh parsley
1/2 teaspoon pepper
1 bay leaf
1 medium potato, boiled, peeled
  and mashed (about 2/3 cup)
1 cup all-purpose flour
1 jumbo egg

Heat oil in 4-quart Dutch oven over medium-high heat. Sauté garlic and onion in oil. Stir in chicken livers; cook over medium heat about 5 minutes, stirring frequently, until livers are brown. Stir in chicken broth, water, wine, parsley, pepper and bay leaf. Heat to boiling; reduce heat. Simmer uncovered 40 minutes.

Mix potato, flour and egg. Shape mixture into 1-inch balls. (Coat hands with flour, if necessary, to prevent sticking.) Remove bay leaf from soup. Heat soup to boiling; add dumplings. When dumplings rise to the surface, boil 4 minutes longer.   **6 servings**

PER SERVING: Calories 255; Protein 19 g; Carbohydrate 24 g; Fat 9 g; Cholesterol 340 mg; Sodium 560 mg

Chicken and Corn Chowder

This Pennsylvania Dutch recipe is thick with diced chicken, tender corn kernels and rivels, *diminutive dumplings.*

3- to 3 1/2-pound broiler-fryer chicken, cut
  up
6 cups water
1 medium onion, sliced
3 medium stalks celery (with leaves),
  finely chopped (about 1 1/2 cups)
1 medium carrot, chopped (about 1/2 cup)
2 teaspoons salt
1 can (17 ounces) cream-style corn
2 hard-cooked eggs, finely chopped
Egg Rivels (below)

Remove any excess fat from chicken. Place chicken, giblets (except liver) and neck in Dutch oven. Add water, onion, celery, carrot and salt; heat to boiling. Skim foam from broth; reduce heat. Cover and simmer about 1 1/2 hours or until thickest pieces of chicken are done.

Remove chicken from broth; cool chicken about 10 minutes or just until cool enough to handle. Remove chicken from bones and skin; cut chicken into small pieces. Skim fat from broth; return chicken to broth. Stir in corn and eggs. Heat to boiling; reduce heat. Prepare Egg Rivels. Sprinkle chicken with Egg Rivel mixture; stir into soup. Simmer uncovered 10 minutes.

                                        8 servings

PER SERVING: Calories 345; Protein 38 g; Carbohydrate 28 g; Fat 9 g; Cholesterol 170; Sodium 930 mg

Egg Rivels

1 cup all-purpose flour
1/4 teaspoon salt
1 egg

Mix all ingredients until mixture looks like cornmeal.

Chicken and Corn Chowder

Wonton Soup

¼ **pound raw medium shrimp (in shells)**
2 **ounces lean ground pork**
3 **whole water chestnuts, finely chopped**
2 **green onions (with tops), chopped**
1 **teaspoon cornstarch**
½ **teaspoon salt**
¼ **teaspoon sesame oil**
Dash of white pepper
24 **wonton skins**
1 **egg white, slightly beaten**
5 **cups water**
½ **chicken breast (about ½ pound)**
½ **teaspoon cornstarch**
½ **teaspoon salt**
Dash of white pepper
4 **ounces Chinese pea pods**
4 **ounces mushrooms**
4 **cups chicken broth**
¼ **cup sliced canned bamboo shoots**
1 **teaspoon salt**
Dash of white pepper
2 **tablespoons chopped green onions**
   (with tops)
¼ **teaspoon sesame oil**

Peel shrimp. Make a shallow cut lengthwise down back of each shrimp; wash out vein. Chop shrimp finely. Mix shrimp, pork, water chestnuts, 2 green onions, 1 teaspoon cornstarch, ½ teaspoon salt, ¼ teaspoon sesame oil and dash of white pepper.

Place ½ teaspoon shrimp mixture in center of wonton skin. (Cover remaining skins with plastic wrap to keep them pliable.) Fold bottom corner of wonton skin over filling to opposite corner, forming a triangle. Brush right corner of triangle with egg white. Bring corners together below filling; pinch left corner to right corner to seal. Repeat with remaining wonton skins. (Cover filled wontons with plastic wrap to keep them from drying out.)

Heat water to boiling in Dutch oven; add wontons. Heat to boiling; reduce heat. Simmer uncovered 2 minutes; drain. Rinse wontons under cold water; place in bowl and cover with iced water to keep them from sticking together.

Remove bones and skin from chicken breast; cut chicken into thin slices. Toss chicken, ½ teaspoon cornstarch, ½ teaspoon salt and dash of white pepper in medium bowl. Cover and refrigerate 20 minutes. Remove strings from pea pods. Place pea pods in boiling water. Cover and cook 1 minute; drain. Immediately rinse in cold water; drain. Cut pea pods lengthwise into halves. Cut mushrooms into ¼-inch slices.

Heat broth and mushrooms to boiling in Dutch oven. Stir in chicken; heat to boiling. Drain wontons. Stir wontons, bamboo shoots, 1 teaspoon salt and dash of white pepper into broth. Heat to boiling; reduce heat. Simmer uncovered 2 minutes. Stir in pea pods, 2 tablespoons green onions and ¼ teaspoon sesame oil.

8 servings

PER SERVING: Calories 160; Protein 10 g; Carbohydrate 19 g; Fat 5 g; Cholesterol 25 mg; Sodium 1060 mg

Chicken and Dumplings

3- to 3½-pound stewing chicken, cut up
4 celery stalk tops
1 medium carrot, sliced
1 small onion, sliced
2 sprigs fresh parsley, snipped
1 teaspoon salt
⅛ teaspoon pepper
5 cups water
2½ cups Bisquick®
⅔ cup milk

Remove any excess fat from chicken. Place chicken, giblets (except liver), neck, celery, carrot, onion, parsley, salt, pepper and water in Dutch oven. Cover and heat to boiling; reduce heat. Cook over low heat about 2 hours or until chicken is done. Remove chicken and vegetables. Skim ½ cup fat from broth; reserve. Remove broth; reserve 4 cups. Heat reserved fat in Dutch oven; blend in ½ cup baking mix. Cook over low heat, stirring constantly, until mixture is smooth and bubbly; remove from heat. Stir in reserved broth. Heat to boiling, stirring constantly. Boil and stir 1 minute. Return chicken and vegetables to Dutch oven; heat through.

Mix 2 cups baking mix and the milk until soft dough forms. Drop by spoonfuls onto hot chicken mixture. Cook uncovered over low heat 10 minutes; cover and cook 10 minutes longer.

4 to 6 servings

PER SERVING: Calories 655; Protein 47 g; Carbohydrate 51 g; Fat 29 g; Cholesterol 130 mg; Sodium 1750 mg

Mulligatawny Soup

Mulligatawny is an Indian spicy soup adapted to British tastes. Cloves and mace add a deep note to this chicken-filled broth.

2½- to 3-pound broiler-fryer chicken, cut up
4 cups water
1½ teaspoons salt
1 teaspoon curry powder
1 teaspoon lemon juice
⅛ teaspoon ground cloves
⅛ teaspoon ground mace
1 medium onion, chopped (about ½ cup)
2 tablespoons margarine or butter
2 tablespoons all-purpose flour
1 medium carrot, thinly sliced
1 apple, chopped
1 medium green bell pepper, cut into ½-inch pieces
2 medium tomatoes, chopped
Parsley

Heat chicken, water, salt, curry powder, lemon juice, cloves and mace to boiling in Dutch oven; reduce heat. Cover and simmer until thickest pieces of chicken are done, about 45 minutes. Remove chicken and broth; skim fat from broth if necessary. Add enough water to broth, if necessary, to measure 4 cups. Remove bones and skin from chicken; cut chicken into pieces.

Cook and stir onion in margarine in Dutch oven until tender. Remove from heat; stir in flour. Gradually stir in broth. Add chicken, carrot, apple, bell pepper and tomatoes. Heat to boiling; reduce heat. Cover and simmer until carrot is tender, about 10 minutes. Serve in shallow soup bowls; garnish with parsley. **6 servings**

PER SERVING: Calories 195; Protein 20 g; Carbohydrate 11 g; Fat 8 g; Cholesterol 55 mg; Sodium 640 mg

Chicken and Vegetable Stew

This flavorful Caribbean stew is spiced with a hot chili and chock full of such tempting vegetables as sweet potatoes, sweet corn and winter squash. It is especially popular in the Dominican Republic.

2½- to 3-pound broiler-fryer chicken,
   cut up
6 cups water
2 tablespoons instant beef bouillon
2 medium tomatoes, chopped
2 medium onions, chopped
2 medium potatoes, cut into ½-inch
   slices
2 medium sweet potatoes or yams, cut
   into ½-inch slices
3 ears sweet corn, cut into 3 pieces
¼ pound winter squash, pared and cut
   into ½-inch pieces (about 1 cup)
½ cup fresh or frozen green peas
1 small hot chili, stemmed, seeded and
   sliced
2 teaspoons salt
¼ teaspoon pepper
Snipped chives

Heat chicken, water and bouillon (dry) to boiling in Dutch oven; reduce heat. Cover and simmer 30 minutes. Skim off fat. Add remaining ingredients except chives. Heat to boiling; reduce heat. Cover and simmer until thickest pieces of chicken are done and vegetables are tender, about 20 minutes. Garnish each serving with chives. **8 or 9 servings**

PER SERVING: Calories 290; Protein 30 g; Carbohydrate 29 g; Fat 6 g; Cholesterol 75 mg; Sodium 640 mg

Soup Garnishes

Soup is delicious on its own, but garnishes can add a special flavor or texture. Try some of these garnishes on your soups:

• Lemon or lime slices or zest
• Bell pepper rings
• Sliced green onions
• Thinly sliced carrots
• Croutons
• Crackers, oyster crackers, corn chips
• Popcorn
• Sprigs or snipped parsley or dill
• Paprika
• Toasted nuts
• Shredded cheese
• Hard-cooked eggs—sliced, crumbled or chopped
• Cooked, crumbled bacon
• Sour cream, whipped cream or yogurt

Brunswick Stew

Once prepared with squirrel and other small woodland animals this rustic stew evolved into a dish usually made with chicken or turkey and a variety of vegetables.

3- to 3½-pound broiler-fryer chicken, cut up
2 cups water
1 teaspoon salt
¼ teaspoon pepper
Dash of ground red pepper (cayenne)
2 cans (16 ounces each) whole tomatoes, undrained
1 can (17 ounces) whole kernel corn, undrained
1 can (14 ounces) lima beans, undrained
1 medium potato, cut into cubes (about 1 cup)
1 medium onion, chopped (about ½ cup)
¼ pound lean salt pork, cut into 1-inch pieces
½ cup water
2 tablespoons all-purpose flour

Remove any excess fat from chicken. Heat chicken, giblets (except liver), neck, 2 cups water and the salt to boiling in Dutch oven; reduce heat. Cover and simmer about 1 hour or until thickest pieces of chicken are done.

Remove chicken from broth; cool chicken about 10 minutes or just until cool enough to handle. Skim fat from broth. Remove skin and bones from chicken if desired; return chicken to broth. Stir in pepper, red pepper, tomatoes, corn, beans, potato, onion and salt pork. Heat to boiling; reduce heat. Simmer uncovered 1 hour. Shake ½ cup water and the flour in tightly covered container. Stir into stew. Heat to boiling, stirring constantly. Boil and stir 1 minute.

8 servings

PER SERVING: Calories 325; Protein 24 g; Carbohydrate 30 g; Fat 12 g; Cholesterol 55 mg; Sodium 880 mg

Chicken Breasts in Lemon-Caper Sauce

3

Stovetop Favorites

Chicken Breasts in Lemon-Caper Sauce

4 skinless boneless chicken
  breast halves (about 1½
  pounds)
½ cup all-purpose flour
¼ cup butter or margarine
2 teaspoons chopped garlic
1 cup dry white wine or chicken broth
2 tablespoons lemon juice
½ teaspoon pepper
1 tablespoon large capers,
  drained
Strawberries
Parsley sprigs

Cut each chicken breast horizontally to make 2 thin slices. Coat with flour. Heat margarine in 12-inch skillet over medium-high heat. Cook chicken and garlic in butter 4 to 6 minutes, turning once, until chicken is brown. Add wine and lemon juice; sprinkle with pepper. Heat until hot. Sprinkle with capers. Garnish with strawberries and parsley. **4 servings**

PER SERVING: Calories 360; Protein 39 g; Carbohydrate 15 g; Fat 16 g; Cholesterol 125 mg; Sodium 170 mg

Chicken with White Wine Sauce

4 skinless boneless chicken breast
  halves (about 1½ pounds)
1 tablespoon vegetable oil
½ cup whipping cream
¼ cup dry white wine or chicken broth
1 teaspoon Dijon mustard
½ teaspoon salt
6 green onions (with tops), cut into 1-
  inch pieces

Cut each chicken breast half lengthwise into 3 pieces. Cook chicken in oil in 10-inch skillet over medium heat, turning occasionally, until white. Stir in remaining ingredients.

Heat to boiling over medium-high heat. Continue boiling, stirring occasionally, until sauce is slightly thickened, about 15 minutes. Garnish with green onion tops, cut into thin slices.

6 servings

PER SERVING: Calories 225; Protein 25 g; Carbohydrate 2 g; Fat 13 g; Cholesterol 90 mg; Sodium 260 mg

Chicken Breasts with Sun-dried–Tomato Sauce

Use plain sun-dried tomatoes rather than those packed in oil.

¼ cup coarsely chopped sun-dried
   tomatoes
½ cup chicken broth
4 skinless boneless chicken breast
   halves (about 1 pound)
½ cup sliced fresh mushrooms (about 1½
   ounces)
2 tablespoons chopped green onions
   (with tops)
2 cloves garlic, finely chopped
2 tablespons dry red wine or chicken
   broth
1 teaspoon vegetable oil
½ cup skim milk
2 teaspoons cornstarch
2 teaspoons chopped fresh or ½ teaspoon
   dried basil leaves
2 cups hot cooked fettuccine or rice

Mix tomatoes and broth; let stand 30 minutes.

Trim fat from chicken. Cook mushrooms, onions and garlic in wine in 10-inch nonstick skillet over medium heat about 3 minutes, stirring occasionally, until mushrooms are tender; remove mixture from skillet. Add oil to skillet. Cook chicken in oil over medium heat until brown on both sides. Add tomato mixture. Heat to boiling; reduce heat. Cover and simmer about 10 minutes, stirring occasionally, until chicken is done. Remove chicken; keep warm. Mix milk, cornstarch and basil; stir into tomato mixture. Heat to boiling, stirring constantly. Boil and stir 1 minute. Stir In mushroom mixture; heat through. Serve over chicken and fettuccine.   **4 servings**

PER SERVING: Calories 345; Protein 46 g; Carbohydrate 28 g; Fat 4 g; Cholesterol 100 mg; Sodium 240 mg

MICROWAVE DIRECTIONS: Decrease broth to ¼ cup. Omit oil. Decrease milk to ¼ cup. Mix tomatoes and broth as directed. Trim fat from chicken. Place mushrooms, onions, garlic and wine in 4-cup microwavable measure. Cover tightly and microwave on high 2 to 3 minutes or until mushrooms are tender; reserve. Place chicken in 2-quart microwavable casserole. Pour tomato mixture over chicken. Cover tightly and microwave on high 10 to 12 minutes, rotating casserole ¼ turn every 3 minutes, until chicken is done. Remove chicken; keep warm. Mix milk, cornstarch and basil; stir into tomato mixture. Microwave uncovered 2 to 4 minutes, stirring every minute, until mixture thickens and boils. Stir in mushroom mixture. Microwave uncovered 30 to 60 seconds or until mixture boils. Serve over chicken and fettuccine.

Chicken Breasts with Sun-dried-Tomato Sauce

Sherried Orange Chicken

4 small chicken breast halves
(about 2 pounds), skinned and boned
2 tablespoons sherry
2 tablespoons soy sauce
1 tablespoon packed brown sugar
1 teaspoon snipped fresh or ¼ teaspoon
dried oregano leaves
2 cloves garlic, finely chopped
1 can (11 ounces) mandarin orange segments, drained (reserve juice)
1 teaspoon vegetable oil
2 teaspoons cornstarch
2 tablespoons raisins
2 cups hot cooked rice
1 tablespoon snipped fresh chives

Remove excess fat from chicken. Place chicken breasts in glass or plastic bowl or heavy plastic bag. Mix sherry, soy sauce, brown sugar, oregano, garlic and ¼ cup of the reserved mandarin orange juice; pour over chicken. Cover and refrigerate 1 hour, turning once.

Heat oil in 10-inch nonstick skillet until hot. Cook chicken in oil over medium heat until lightly browned on both sides; add sherry mixture. Reduce heat; cover and cook until chicken is done, about 10 minutes. Remove chicken; keep warm. Mix cornstarch and remaining juice; stir into hot liquid. Heat to boiling, stirring constantly. Boil and stir 1 minute. Stir in orange segments and raisins; heat through. Serve chicken and sauce over rice; sprinkle with chives. **4 servings**

PER SERVING: Calories 365; Protein 36 g; Carbohydrate 42 g; Fat 5 g; Cholesterol 85 mg; Sodium 970 mg

Chicken in Red Wine Vinegar

2 tablespoons margarine or butter
2 cloves garlic, crushed
3 shallots, chopped
6 skinless boneless chicken breast
halves (about 2¼ pounds)
½ cup red wine vinegar
2 cups finely chopped tomato
(about 2 medium tomatoes)
2 teaspoons chopped fresh or ½ teaspoon dried thyme leaves
½ teaspoon salt
¼ teaspoon pepper

Melt margarine in 10-inch skillet. Add garlic, shallots and chicken. Cook over medium-high heat 12 to 15 minutes, turning after 6 minutes, until chicken is no longer pink. Reduce heat to low. Add vinegar; cover and cook 5 minutes. Stir in remaining ingredients; turn chicken. Cook over low heat 10 to 12 minutes until chicken is done. **6 servings**

PER SERVING: Calories 250; Protein 37 g; Carbohydrate 5 g; Fat 9 g; Cholesterol 95 mg; Sodium 300 mg

Chicken Cordon Bleu

2 whole chicken breasts (about 1½ pounds)
4 thin slices fully cooked smoked ham or
  prosciutto
4 thin slices Swiss cheese
¼ cup all-purpose flour
¼ teaspoon salt
¼ teaspoon pepper
1 egg, slightly beaten
½ cup dry bread crumbs
3 tablespoons vegetable oil
2 tablespoons water

Remove bones and skin from chicken breasts. Cut chicken breasts into halves. Flatten each half to ¼-inch thickness between plastic wrap or waxed paper. Place 1 slice ham and 1 slice cheese on each chicken breast. Roll up carefully, beginning at narrow end. Secure with wooden picks. Mix flour, salt and pepper. Coat rolls with flour mixture. Dip rolls into egg and roll in bread crumbs.

Heat oil in 10-inch skillet over medium heat. Cook rolls in oil 5 to 10 minutes, turning occasionally, until light brown. Add water. Cover and simmer about 10 minutes or until juices run clear. Remove wooden picks.   **4 servings**

PER SERVING: Calories 445; Protein 40 g; Carbohydrate 16 g; Fat 23 g; Cholesterol 170 mg; Sodium 560 mg

MICROWAVE DIRECTIONS: Omit vegetable oil and water. Place chicken, seam sides up, on microwavable rack in rectangular microwavable dish, 11 × 7 × 1½ inches. Cover with waxed paper and microwave on high 6 to 8 minutes or until juices run clear. Remove wooden picks.

Spicy Chicken with Broccoli

2 whole chicken breasts (about 2
  pounds)
2 teaspoons cornstarch
½ teaspoon salt
¼ teaspoon white pepper
1 pound broccoli
3 green onions (with tops)
1 hot green chili or 1 teaspoon dried red
  pepper flakes
3 tablespoons vegetable oil
2 tablespoons brown bean sauce
2 teaspoons finely chopped garlic
1 teaspoon sugar
1 teaspoon finely chopped gingerroot

Remove bones and skin from chicken breasts; cut chicken into 2 × ½-inch pieces. Toss chicken, cornstarch, salt and white pepper in medium bowl. Cover and refrigerate 20 minutes.

Pare outer layer from broccoli. Cut broccoli lengthwise into 1-inch-thick stems; remove flowerets. Cut stems diagonally into ¼-inch slices. Place broccoli flowerets and stems in boiling water; heat to boiling. Cover and cook 1 minute; drain. Immediately rinse in cold water; drain. Cut green onions diagonally into 1-inch pieces. Remove seeds and membranes from chili. Cut chili into very thin slices.

Heat wok until very hot. Add 3 tablespoons vegetable oil; tilt wok to coat side. Add chili, brown bean sauce, garlic, sugar and gingerroot; stir-fry 10 seconds. Add chicken; stir-fry 2 minutes or until chicken is white. Add broccoli and green onions; stir-fry 1 minute or until broccoli is hot.   **4 servings**

PER SERVING: Calories 330; Protein 39 g; Carbohydrate 10 g; Fat 15 g; Cholesterol 90 mg; Sodium 710 mg

Sesame Chicken with Fun See

Sesame Chicken with Fun See

The quickly fried cellophane noodles here (fun see) add crunch to this hot-and-sour dish.

2 whole chicken breasts (about 2 pounds)
1 egg
2 tablespoons all-purpose flour
2 tablespoons cornstarch
2 tablespoons water
1 teaspoon salt
2 teaspoons vegetable oil
¼ teaspoon baking soda
¼ teaspoon white pepper
½ cup water
¼ cup cornstarch
1 cup sugar
1 cup chicken broth
¾ cup vinegar
2 teaspoons dark soy sauce
2 teaspoons chili paste
1 teaspoon vegetable oil
1 clove garlic, finely chopped
Vegetable oil
2 ounces cellophane or rick stick noodles
2 tablespoons toasted sesame seed (see Note)

Remove bones and skin from chicken breasts; cut chicken into 2 × ½-inch strips. Mix egg, flour, 2 tablespoons cornstarch, 2 tablespoons water, the salt, 2 teaspoons vegetable oil, the baking soda and white pepper; stir in chicken. Cover and refrigerate 20 minutes. Mix ½ cup water and ¼ cup cornstarch

Heat sugar, broth, vinegar, soy sauce, chili paste, 1 teaspoon vegetable oil and the garlic to boiling. Stir in cornstarch mixture; cook and stir until thickened. Remove from heat; keep warm.

Heat vegetable oil (1½ inches) in wok to 350°. Pull noodles apart gently. Fry ¼ of the noodles at a time 5 seconds or until puffed, turning once; drain on paper towels.

Heat oil to 350°. Fry about 10 pieces of chicken, adding 1 at a time, 3 minutes or until light brown. Remove from oil, using slotted spoon; drain on paper towels. Repeat with remaining chicken.

Heat oil to 375°. Fry about ⅓ of the chicken 1 minute or until golden brown. Remove from oil, using slotted spoon; drain on paper towels. Repeat with remaining chicken. Place chicken on heated platter.

Heat sauce to boiling; pour over chicken. Sprinkle with sesame seed. Arrange cellophane noodles around chicken. **6 servings**

PER SERVING: Calories 445; Protein 26 g; Carbohydrate 49 g; Fat 16 g; Cholesterol 60 mg; Sodium 710 mg.

NOTE: To toast sesame seed, heat 8-inch skillet until hot; reduce heat to medium low. Add sesame seed; cook and stir until sesame seed is brown, about 2 minutes.

Stir-frying Tips

Stir-fried foods are cooked very quickly in a small amount of oil over very high heat. Vegetable oil or peanut oil, with a high smoking point, does the job best. Because of its sloping sides and rounded bottom, a wok is the ideal utensil; however, a deep skillet with sloping sides can be used. Be sure to keep the food moving constantly. Using a wide spatula or long-handled spoon, bring it down the side and across the bottom, lifting and turning the food.

Walnut Chicken

Use a paring knife to loosen and remove skins from blanched walnuts. The walnuts must be hot for the skins to come off easily.

2 cups water
1 cup walnuts
¼ teaspoon sugar
2 whole chicken breasts (about 2 pounds)
1 egg white
2 teaspoons cornstarch
1 teaspoon salt
⅛ teaspoon white pepper
2 ounces Chinese pea pods
2 stalks celery
2 green onions (with tops)
2 tablespoons oyster sauce
1 tablespoon cornstarch
1 tablespoon water
1 cup vegetable oil
½ cup chicken broth
1 tablespoon diced pimiento

Heat 2 cups water to boiling; add walnuts. Heat to boiling; boil 1 minute. Drain; rinse under cold water. Remove skin from walnuts; sprinkle walnuts with sugar.

Remove bones and skin from chicken breasts; cut chicken into ¾-inch pieces. Mix egg white, 2 teaspoons cornstarch, the salt and white pepper in medium bowl; stir in chicken. Cover and refrigerate 20 minutes.

Remove strings from pea pods; cut large pea pods into 3 pieces. Place pea pods in boiling water; heat to boiling. Boil 30 seconds; drain. Immediately rinse in cold water. Cut celery diagonally into ¼-inch slices. Cut green onions diagonally into 1-inch pieces. Mix oyster sauce, 1 tablespoon cornstarch and 1 tablespoon water.

Heat vegetable oil in wok to 350°. Add walnuts; fry until walnuts are light brown. Remove walnuts from oil, using slotted spoon; drain on paper towels.

Heat vegetable oil to 350°. Add chicken; fry until chicken turns white, stirring to separate pieces. Remove chicken from oil, using slotted spoon; drain on paper towels. Pour oil from wok, reserving 2 tablespoons.

Heat wok until very hot. Add 2 tablespoons reserved vegetable oil; tilt wok to coat side. Add celery; stir-fry 1 minute. Add broth; heat to boiling. Cover and simmer 1 minute. Add chicken, pea pods, green onions and pimiento; heat to boiling. Stir in cornstarch mixture; cook and stir until mixture thickens. Stir in walnuts.

4 servings

PER SERVING: Calories 585; Protein 42 g; Carbohydrate 12 g; Fat 41 g; Cholesterol 90 mg; Sodium 1090 mg

Sichuan Chicken with Cashews

In this recipe, the method of coating chicken pieces in a cornstarch batter and then stir-frying them twice produces well-sealed, tender morsels. You'll find raw cashews are readily available in health-food stores or Oriental markets.

2 whole chicken breasts (about 2 pounds)
1 egg white
1 teaspoon cornstarch
1 teaspoon soy sauce
Dash of white pepper
1 large green bell pepper
1 medium onion
1 can (8½ ounces) sliced bamboo shoots, drained
1 tablespoon cornstarch
1 tablespoon cold water
1 tablespoon soy sauce
2 tablespoons vegetable oil
1 cup raw cashews
¼ teaspoon salt
2 tablespoons vegetable oil
1 teaspoon finely chopped gingerroot
1 tablespoon Hoisin sauce
2 teaspoons chili paste
¼ cup chicken broth
2 tablespoons chopped green onions (with tops)

Remove bones and skin from chicken breasts; cut chicken into ¾-inch pieces. Mix egg white, 1 teaspoon cornstarch, 1 teaspoon soy sauce and the white pepper in medium bowl; stir in chicken. Cover and refrigerate 20 minutes.

Cut bell pepper into ¾-inch pieces. Cut onion into 8 pieces. Cut bamboo shoots into ½-inch pieces. Mix 1 tablespoon cornstarch, the water and 1 tablespoon soy sauce.

Heat wok until very hot. Add 2 tablespoons vegetable oil; tilt wok to coat side. And cashews; stir-fry 1 minute or until cashews are light brown. Remove cashews from wok; drain on paper towel. Sprinkle with salt. Add chicken to wok; stir-fry until chicken turns white. Remove chicken from wok.

Add 2 tablespoons vegetable oil; tilt wok to coat side. Add onion pieces and gingerroot; stir-fry until gingerroot is light brown. Add chicken, bell pepper, bamboo shoots, Hoisin sauce and chili paste; stir-fry 1 minute. Add broth; heat to boiling. Stir in cornstarch mixture; cook and stir 20 seconds or until thickened. Stir in cashews and green onions. **4 servings**

PER SERVING: Calories 575; Protein 44 g; Carbohydrate 21 g; Fat 35 g; Cholesterol 90 mg; Sodium 1040 mg

Lemon Chicken

After frying, you can refrigerate the chicken for 24 hours if you choose. Make the sauce ahead, too, if it's more convenient. Just before serving, heat oil to 375° and fry chicken, turning once or twice, for about 2 minutes. Reheat sauce to boiling and serve over chicken.

2 whole chicken breasts (about 2 pounds)
1 egg
2 teaspoons cornstarch
1 teaspoon salt
1/4 teaspoon white pepper
1 teaspoon finely chopped gingerroot
1 tablespoon cornstarch
1 tablespoon water
Vegetable oil
1/4 cup all-purpose flour
1/4 cup water
2 tablespoons cornstarch
2 tablespoons vegetable oil
1/4 teaspoon baking soda
1/4 teaspoon salt
1/3 cup chicken broth
1/4 cup sugar
3 tablespoons lemon juice
2 tablespoons light corn syrup
2 tablespoons vinegar
1 tablespoon vegetable oil
1 teaspoon dark soy sauce
1 teaspoon finely chopped garlic
1/2 lemon, thinly sliced

Remove bones and skin from chicken breasts; cut each chicken breast lengthwise into fourths. Place chicken in a shallow dish. Mix egg, 2 teaspoons cornstarch, 1 teaspoon salt, the white pepper and gingerroot. Pour egg mixture over chicken, turning chicken to coat all sides. Cover and refrigerate 30 minutes. Remove chicken from marinade; reserve marinade. Mix 1 tablespoon cornstarch and 1 tablespoon water; set aside.

Heat vegetable oil (1½ inches) in wok to 350°. Mix reserved marinade, the flour, 1/4 cup water, 2 tablespoons cornstarch, 2 tablespoons vegetable oil, the baking soda and 1/4 teaspoon salt. Dip chicken pieces, one at a time, into batter to coat all sides. Fry 2 pieces at a time 3 minutes or until light brown; drain on paper towels.

Increase oil temperature to 375°. Fry all the chicken 2 minutes or until golden brown, turning once; drain on paper towels. Cut each piece crosswise into ½-inch pieces, using a very sharp knife; place in a single layer on heated platter.

Heat broth, sugar, lemon juice, corn syrup, vinegar, 1 tablespoon vegetable oil, the soy sauce and garlic to boiling. Stir in reserved cornstarch mixture; cook and stir 10 seconds or until thickened. Simmer uncovered 30 seconds. Pour sauce over chicken; garnish with lemon slices and, if desired, maraschino cherries or cilantro.

6 servings

PER SERVING: Calories 375; Protein 26 g; Carbohydrate 23 g; Fat 20 g; Cholesterol 95 mg; Sodium 650 mg

Orange-glazed Chicken and Carrots

1 package (6¾ ounces) instant long grain and wild rice
1 tablespoon vegetable oil
2 large skinless boneless chicken breast halves (about ¾ pound), cut into 1½-inch pieces
1 package (16 ounces) frozen whole baby carrots
1 can (6 ounces) frozen orange juice concentrate, thawed
1 juice can water
2 tablespoons honey
2 tablespoons cornstarch
1 teaspoon dry mustard
2 tablespoons cold water

Prepare instant rice as directed on package; keep warm. Heat oil in 10-inch skillet over medium heat until hot. Cook and stir chicken in oil until white.

Stir in carrots, orange juice, juice can water and honey. Heat to boiling; reduce heat to medium. Cook uncovered, stirring occasionally, until carrots are done, 10 to 12 minutes.

Mix cornstarch and mustard; stir in cold water. Stir into chicken mixture. Heat to boiling, stirring constantly. Boil and stir 1 minute. Serve with rice. **4 servings**

PER SERVING: Calories 470; Protein 25 g; Carbohydrate 77 g; Fat 7 g; Cholesterol 45 mg; Sodium 120 mg

Raspberry-Peach Chicken

Fresh fruit adds flavor—but not a lot of calories—to this dish.

½ cup fresh or frozen raspberries
1 small peach, peeled and sliced
2 tablespoons peach brandy or apple juice
2 tablespoons honey
¼ cup all-purpose flour
¼ teaspoon salt
¼ teaspoon pepper
4 skinless boneless chicken breast halves (about 1 pound)
1 tablespoon vegetable oil

Place raspberries, peach slices, brandy and honey in blender or food processor. Cover and blend on high speed or process about 1 minute or until smooth. Heat in 1-quart saucepan over medium heat until hot, stirring occasionally. Keep warm.

Mix flour, salt and pepper. Coat chicken breast halves with flour mixture. Heat oil in 10-inch skillet. Cook chicken over medium heat 12 to 14 minutes, turning once, until juices of chicken run clear. Serve chicken with sauce. Garnish with additional raspberries, and serve with rice if desired. **4 servings**

PER SERVING: Calories 255; Protein 27 g; Carbohydrate 19 g; Fat 5 g; Cholesterol 19 mg; Sodium 210 mg

Chicken-Chutney Stir-Fry

Chicken-Chutney Stir-Fry

1 tablespoon vegetable oil
3 skinless boneless chicken breast
   halves (about 1 pound), cut into 1-inch
   pieces
2 carrots, thinly sliced (about 1 cup)
½ medium red bell pepper, cut into thin
   strips
1 tablespoon cornstarch
1 tablespoon soy sauce
½ cup chutney
6 ounces pea pods
¼ cup chopped peanuts

Heat oil in 10-inch skillet or wok until hot. Add chicken, carrots and bell pepper. Stir-fry over medium-high heat 5 to 7 minutes or until chicken is white. Mix cornstarch, soy sauce and chutney. Stir into chicken mixture. Cook and stir over medium heat until slightly thickened. Stir in pea pods; heat until hot. Serve over rice. Sprinkle with peanuts. **4 servings**

PER SERVING: Calories 310; Protein 29 g; Carbohydrate 24 g; Fat 11 g; Cholesterol 60 mg; Sodium 380 mg

Italian Chicken Stir-Fry

Pepperoni cut into strips rather than left in slices makes that marvelous flavor go further.

1 pound skinless boneless chicken
   breasts
1 tablespoon olive or vegetable oil
¼ cup ¼-inch strips thinly sliced pepperoni (about 1 ounce)
2 cloves garlic, finely chopped
2 large bell peppers, cut into 1-inch
   squares
1 medium onion, thinly sliced
2 cups ¼-inch zucchini slices (about 2
   medium)
¼ cup dry red wine
1 teaspoon snipped fresh thyme leaves
   or ½ teaspoon dried thyme leaves
1 teaspoon snipped fresh rosemary
   leaves or ½ teaspoon dried rosemary
   leaves
¼ teaspoon salt
⅛ teaspoon pepper
1 tablespoon grated Parmesan cheese

Remove excess fat from chicken; cut chicken into 2-inch pieces. Heat oil in 10-inch nonstick skillet or wok over medium-high heat. Add chicken, pepperoni and garlic; stir-fry until chicken is almost done, 3 to 4 minutes. Remove chicken mixture from skillet; keep warm.

Heat remaining ingredients except cheese to boiling in skillet; stir-fry until vegetables are crisp-tender, 3 to 4 minutes. Stir in chicken; heat through. Sprinkle with Parmesan cheese.
4 servings

PER SERVING: Calories 290; Protein 37 g; Carbohydrate 10 g; Fat 10 g; Cholesterol 95 mg; Sodium 370 mg

Spicy Curried Chicken with Couscous

**4 small chicken breast halves
    (about 2 pounds), skinned and boned**
2 teaspoons vegetable oil
¼ teaspoon salt
⅛ teaspoon ground red pepper (cayenne)
1 teaspoon vegetable oil
**1 cup chopped unpared green apple
    (about 1 medium)**
½ cup chopped onion (about 1 medium)
1 clove garlic, finely chopped
2 teaspoons curry powder
2 teaspoons grated orange peel
1 cup chicken broth or water
¼ cup raisins
1 tablespoon cornstarch
¼ cup cold water
2 cups hot cooked couscous or rice

Remove excess fat from chicken; cut chicken into 1-inch pieces. Heat 2 teaspoons oil in 10-inch nonstick skillet until hot. Cook and stir chicken, salt and red pepper in oil over medium heat until chicken is done, about 5 minutes; remove chicken. Add 1 teaspoon oil, the apple, onion, garlic, curry powder and orange peel; cook and stir until apple is tender, about 7 minutes.

Stir in chicken broth, raisins and chicken. Heat to boiling, stirring constantly. Mix cornstarch and water; stir into chicken mixture. Boil and stir 1 minute. Serve on couscous.   **4 servings**

PER SERVING: Calories 385; Protein 37 g; Carbohydrate 42 g; Fat 7 g; Cholesterol 85 mg; Sodium 790 mg

Curried Chicken and Nectarines

**4 skinless boneless chicken breast
    halves (about 1 pound)**
**2 tablespoons reduced-calorie oil-and-
    vinegar dressing**
1 teaspoon curry powder
¼ cup raisins
¼ cup sliced green onions (with tops)
¼ teaspoon salt
**1 medium bell pepper, cut into ¼-inch
    strips**
2 small nectarines, cut into ¼-inch slices

Trim fat from chicken breast halves. Cut chicken crosswise into ½-inch strips. Mix dressing and curry powder in medium bowl. Add chicken; toss. Heat 10-inch nonstick skillet over medium-high heat. Stir in chicken and remaining ingredients except nectarines; stir-fry 4 to 6 minutes or until chicken is done. Stir in nectarines carefully; heat through. Serve with hot cooked rice or couscous if desired.   **4 servings**

PER SERVING: Calories 210; Protein 25 g; Carbohydrate 15 g; Fat 6 g; Cholesterol 80 mg; Sodium 230 mg

MICROWAVE DIRECTIONS: Prepare chicken as directed. Mix dressing and curry powder in 2-quart microwavable casserole. Add chicken; toss. Stir in remaining ingredients except nectarines. Cover tightly and microwave on high 8 to 10 minutes, stirring after 4 minutes, until chicken is done. Stir in nectarines carefully. Cover and microwave 1 minute or until heated through.

Curried Chicken and Nectarines

Cold Poached Chicken with Two Sauces

Here is an elegant, do-ahead recipe that is ideal for entertaining. The two southwestern sauces—bright red pepper and pale avocado—are very festive.

4 small chicken breast halves (about 2 pounds), skinned and boned
¼ cup water
1 tablespoon lemon juice
¼ teaspoon salt
Pepper Sauce (below)
Avocado Sauce (right)

Remove excess fat from chicken. Place chicken, water, lemon juice and salt in 10-inch nonstick skillet. Heat to boiling; reduce heat. Cover and simmer until chicken is done, about 10 minutes. Refrigerate until cold, at least 2 hours.

Prepare Pepper Sauce and Avocado Sauce. For each serving, place ¼ cup Pepper Sauce on plate; top with chicken breast half and 2 tablespoons Avocado Sauce.   **4 servings**

PER SERVING: Calories 315; Protein 35 g; Carbohydrate 8 g; Fat 16 g; Cholesterol 100 mg; Sodium 390 mg

Pepper Sauce

2 large red bell peppers
1 jalapeño chile, seeded
1 tablespoon lemon or lime juice
1 tablespoon olive or vegetable oil
¼ teaspoon salt
⅛ teaspoon pepper

Set oven control to broil. Broil bell peppers with tops 4 to 5 inches from heat, turning frequently until skin blisters and browns, about 10 minutes. Wrap in towels and let stand 5 minutes, or place in plastic bag and let stand 15 to 20 minutes. Remove skin, stems, seeds, and membrane from bell peppers. Place bell peppers along with remaining ingredients in blender container. Cover and blend on high speed until smooth, about 15 seconds. Cover and refrigerate.

Avocado Sauce

⅓ cup nonfat plain yogurt
1 tablespoon reduced-calorie sour cream
1 teaspoon lemon juice
½ avocado

Place all ingredients in blender container. Cover and blend on high speed, scraping sides of blender container occasionally, until smooth, about 60 seconds. Cover and refrigerate.

Thai Chicken with Basil

4 skinless boneless chicken breast halves (about 12 ounces)
2 tablespoons vegetable oil
3 cloves garlic, finely chopped
2 red jalapeño peppers, seeded and finely chopped
1 tablespoon fish sauce
1 teaspoon sugar
¼ cup snipped fresh basil leaves
1 tablespoon snipped fresh mint leaves
1 tablespoon chopped unsalted roasted peanuts

Cut each breast half into 4 pieces.

Heat oil in wok or 12-inch skillet until hot. Cook and stir garlic and peppers over medium-high heat until garlic is golden brown. Add chicken; stir-fry until chicken is done, 8 to 10 minutes. Stir in fish sauce and sugar. Sprinkle with remaining ingredients. Garnish with lemon wedges if desired.   **4 servings**

PER SERVING: Calories 195; Protein 20 g; Carbohydrate 6 g; Fat 10 g; Cholesterol 45 mg; Sodium 60 mg

Chicken Tempura

3 or 4 Vegetables (below)
1 large whole chicken breast (about 1 pound), boned, skinned and cut into 1-inch pieces
Vegetable oil
Tempura Batter (right)
Tempura Sauce (right)

Pat vegetables and chicken dry with paper towels. Heat oil (1 to 1½ inches) in wok or electric skillet to 360°. Prepare Tempura Batter. Dip chicken and vegetables into batter with tongs, fork or chopsticks; allow excess batter to drip into bowl. Fry a few pieces at a time, turning once, until golden brown, 2 to 3 minutes; drain. Serve with Tempura Sauce.   **4 servings**

PER SERVING: Calories 440; Protein 34 g; Carbohydrate 31 g; Fat 20 g; Cholesterol 170 mg; Sodium 1500 mg

Vegetables

1½ cups cauliflowerets
1½ cups 2 × ¼-inch strips eggplant
1 cup 1-inch pieces asparagus
1 cup ¼-inch slices carrots or celery
1 cup Chinese pea pods
1 cup 2-inch pieces green beans, partially cooked
1 cup 2-inch pieces green onion
1 medium green pepper, cut into ¼-inch rings
1 medium onion, sliced and separated into rings
1 bunch parsley
1 medium sweet potato, cut into ⅛-inch slices

Tempura Batter

2 eggs
1 cup cold water
¾ cup all-purpose flour
1 tablespoon cornstarch
½ teaspoon baking powder
½ teaspoon salt

Beat eggs; mix in remaining ingredients with fork just until blended. (Batter will be thin and slightly lumpy.)

Tempura Sauce

¼ cup chicken broth
¼ cup water
¼ cup soy sauce
1 teaspoon sugar

Heat all ingredients until hot.

No Chicken?

No need to put off enjoying a favorite recipe. You can substitute cooked turkey or canned chicken in any recipe calling for cut-up cooked chicken. One can (5 ounces) chunk chicken yields about ⅔ cup cut-up cooked chicken.

Chicken-Vegetable Fondue

A Japanese-inspired dish that's also fun to eat!

2 large whole chicken breasts (about 2 pounds), boned, skinned and cut into bite-size pieces
1 pound broccoli, separated into flowerets
8 ounces mushrooms, sliced (about 3 cups)
1 bunch green onions (with tops), cut into ½-inch pieces
4 to 5 cups hot cooked rice
8 cups chicken broth
Lemon-Soy Sauce (below)

Arrange chicken, broccoli, mushrooms and onions on serving tray. Divide rice among 8 small bowls.

Heat broth in electric skillet to 225°. Spear foods with chopsticks or fondue forks and cook in hot broth until done, 2 to 4 minutes, then dip in Lemon-Soy Sauce. At end of main course, ladle broth over rice remaining in bowls and eat as soup. **8 servings**

PER SERVING: Calories 330; Protein 35 g; Carbohydrate 36 g; Fat 5 g; Cholesterol 60 mg; Sodium 1880 mg

Lemon-Soy Sauce

½ cup soy sauce
½ cup lemon juice
¼ cup dry white wine or chicken broth

Mix all ingredients.

Chicken Chili

2 cups cut-up cooked chicken
1 large onion, chopped (about 1 cup)
1 medium green bell pepper, chopped (about 1 cup)
3 to 4 teaspoons chili powder
1 teaspoon salt
¼ teaspoon ground cumin
⅛ teaspoon red pepper sauce
2 cloves garlic, crushed
1 can (16 ounces) whole tomatoes, undrained
1 can (15½ ounces) kidney beans, undrained
1 can (8 ounces) tomato sauce

Heat all ingredients to boiling in 3-quart saucepan; reduce heat. Cover and simmer, stirring occasionally, 20 to 30 minutes. Sprinkle with snipped parsley if desired. **6 servings**

PER SERVING: Calories 295; Protein 34 g; Carbohydrate 24 g; Fat 7 g; Cholesterol 80 mg; Sodium 940 mg

DO-AHEAD NOTE: Omit kidney beans. After simmering mixture, cool quickly and pour into 5- to 6-cup freezer container; cover, label and freeze. About 1 hour before serving, dip container into very hot water just to loosen. Drain kidney beans, reserving liquid. Place reserved bean liquid and frozen block in saucepan. Cover and heat over medium heat, turning block occasionally, until mixture is hot, about 40 minutes. Stir in kidney beans; heat until hot.

Chicken Stroganoff

1 small onion, chopped (about ¼ cup)
1 can (4 ounces) mushroom stems and
   pieces, drained (reserve liquid)
1 tablespoon margarine or butter
⅓ cup milk
½ teaspoon garlic salt
¼ teaspoon pepper
⅛ teaspoon dried thyme leaves
1 can (10¾ ounces) condensed cream of
   chicken or cream of celery soup
2 cups cut-up cooked chicken
¼ cup sliced pimiento-stuffed
   olives
1 package (10 ounces) spinach
   noodles
2 tablespoons margarine or
   butter
1 cup sour cream

Cook and stir onion and mushrooms in 1 tablespoon margarine in 10-inch skillet until onion is
tender, about 5 minutes. Stir in milk, garlic salt,
pepper, thyme, soup and reserved mushroom
liquid. Stir in chicken and olives; heat until hot.

Cook noodles as directed on package; drain.
Toss noodles with 2 tablespoons margarine. Stir
sour cream into chicken mixture; heat just until
hot. Serve over hot noodles and, if desired,
garnish with additional sliced pimiento-stuffed
olives. **6 servings**

PER SERVING: Calories 525; Protein 37 g; Carbohydrate 38 g; Fat 25 g; Cholesterol 150 mg; Sodium 880 mg

Easy Chicken Curry

Get a cooked-all-day taste in just minutes!

2 tablespoons margarine or butter
1 teaspoon curry powder
1 small onion, chopped (about ¼ cup)
2 cups cut-up cooked chicken
⅓ cup raisins
1 small unpared red apple, coarsely
   chopped
1 can (10¾ ounces) condensed cream of
   chicken soup
1 soup can water
2 cups hot cooked rice
Chopped peanuts, if desired

Cook margarine, curry powder and onion in 3-
quart saucepan over medium heat about 4 minutes, stirring frequently, until onion is tender. Stir
in remaining ingredients except rice and peanuts. Cook, stirring occasionally, until hot. Serve
over rice. Sprinkle with peanuts.

4 servings

PER SERVING: Calories 440; Protein 24 g; Carbohydrate 50 g; Fat 15 g; Cholesterol 65 mg; Sodium 110 mg

Chicken and Grape Pilaf

A traditional pilaf calls for cooking rice in hot fat before cooking it in hot broth. This version eliminates that step for a low-fat dish.

  2 cups cubed cooked chicken or turkey
  ¾ cup uncooked regular long grain rice
  ¼ cup sliced green onions (with tops)
  1¾ cups chicken broth
  1 teaspoon margarine
  ¼ teaspoon ground cinnamon
  ¼ teaspoon ground allspice
  ⅛ teaspoon salt
  1 cup seedless grape halves
  2 tablespoons chopped pecans

Heat all ingredients except grape halves and pecans to boiling in 2-quart saucepan, stirring once or twice; reduce heat. Cover and simmer 14 minutes. (Do not lift cover or stir.) Remove from heat. Stir in grape halves and pecans, fluffing rice lightly with fork. Cover and let steam 5 to 10 minutes. **4 servings**

PER SERVING: Calories 210; Protein 23 g; Carbohydrate 8 g; Fat 9 g; Cholesterol 60 mg; Sodium 410 mg

Fried Chicken with Gravy

  2½- to 3-pound broiler-fryer chicken,
    cut up
  ½ cup all-purpose flour
  1 teaspoon salt
  ½ teaspoon paprika
  ¼ teaspoon pepper
  Vegetable oil
  Gravy (below)

Remove any excess fat from chicken. Mix flour, salt, paprika and pepper. Coat chicken with flour mixture. Heat oil (¼ inch) in 10- or 12-inch skillet until hot. Cook chicken in oil over medium heat 15 to 20 minutes or until light brown; reduce heat. Cover tightly and simmer 30 to 40 minutes, turning once or twice, until thickest pieces are done. If skillet cannot be covered tightly, add 1 to 2 tablespoons water. Remove cover during last 5 minutes of cooking to crisp chicken. Serve with Gravy. **4 servings**

PER SERVING: Calories 520; Protein 39 g; Carbohydrate 23 g; Fat 30 g; Cholesterol 110 mg; Sodium 1120 mg

Gravy

  ¼ cup drippings (fat and juices)
  ¼ cup all-purpose flour
  1 cup liquid (meat juices, broth, water)
  1 cup milk
  Salt and pepper to taste

Pour drippings from skillet into bowl, leaving brown particles in skillet. Return ¼ cup drippings to skillet. Stir in flour. Cook over low heat, stirring constantly, until mixture is smooth and bubbly; remove from heat. Stir in liquid and milk. Heat to boiling, stirring constantly. Boil and stir 1 minute. Stir in salt and pepper.

Chicken Paprika with Dumplings

There are many varieties of Hungarian paprika; we recommend using sweet Hungarian paprika in this dish.

2 tablespoons vegetable oil
2½- to 3-pound broiler-fryer chicken,
    cut up
2 medium onions, chopped (about 1 cup)
1 clove garlic, chopped
1 medium tomato, chopped
½ cup water
½ teaspoon instant chicken bouillon
2 tablespoons paprika
1 teaspoon salt
¼ teaspoon pepper
1 medium green bell pepper,
    cut into ½-inch strips
Dumplings (right)
1 cup sour cream

Heat oil in 12-inch skillet until hot. Cook chicken over medium heat until brown on all sides, about 15 minutes. Remove chicken. Cook and stir onions and garlic in oil until onions are tender; drain fat from skillet. Stir in tomato, water, bouillon (dry), paprika, salt and pepper; loosen brown particles from bottom of skillet. Add chicken. Heat to boiling; reduce heat. Cover and simmer 20 minutes. Add bell pepper; cover and cook until thickest pieces of chicken are done, 10 to 15 minutes longer. Prepare Dumplings.

Remove chicken to heated platter; keep warm. Skim fat from skillet. Stir sour cream into liquid in skillet; add Dumplings. Heat just until hot. Serve chicken with Dumplings and sour cream sauce.   **6 to 8 servings**

PER SERVING: Calories 515; Protein 32 g; Carbohydrate 40 g; Fat 25 g; Cholesterol 200 mg; Sodium 1540 mg

Dumplings

8 cups water
1 teaspoon salt
3 eggs, well beaten
½ cup water
2 cups all-purpose flour
2 teaspoons salt

Heat 8 cups water and 1 teaspoon salt to boiling in Dutch oven. Mix eggs, ½ cup water, the flour and 2 teaspoons salt; drop dough by teaspoonfuls into boiling water. Cook uncovered, stirring occasionally, 10 minutes. Drain. (Dumplings will be chewy.)

Brown Chicken Fricassee

Plan on serving lots of fluffy mashed pota- toes or cooked rice to soak up every last bit of this mushroom-rich gravy.

3- to 3½-pound broiler-fryer chicken, cut up
1 cup all-purpose flour
1 teaspoon salt
¼ teaspoon pepper
2 tablespoons vegetable oil
2 cups water
1 cup sliced mushrooms
1 medium onion, chopped (about ½ cup)
2 bay leaves
2 tablespoons all-purpose flour
½ teaspoon salt
3 tablespoons water

Remove any excess fat from chicken. Mix 1 cup flour, 1 teaspoon salt and the pepper. Coat chicken with flour mixture. Heat oil in Dutch oven or 12-inch skillet until hot. Cook chicken in oil over medium-high heat 20 to 25 minutes or until brown. Add 2 cups water, the mushrooms, onion and bay leaves. Cover and cook over low heat 45 to 60 minutes or until thickest pieces of chicken are done.

Remove chicken; keep warm. Mix 2 tablespoons flour, ½ teaspoon salt and 3 tablespoons water in small bowl until smooth; stir into hot liquid. Heat to boiling, stirring constantly. Boil and stir 1 minute; reduce heat. Return chicken to Dutch oven. Cover and simmer 5 minutes. Remove bay leaves. Serve chicken over hot mashed po- tatoes or cooked rice if desired.

6 servings

PER SERVING: Calories 345; Protein 30 g; Carbohy- drate 20 g; Fat 16 g; Cholesterol 85 mg; Sodium 610 mg

Chicken Cacciatore

3- to 3½-pound broiler-fryer chicken, cut up
¼ cup shortening
½ cup all-purpose flour
1 medium green bell pepper
2 medium onions
2 cloves garlic, crushed
1 can (16 ounces) whole tomatoes, drained
1 can (8 ounces) tomato sauce
1 can (4 ounces) sliced mushrooms, drained
½ teaspoon salt
1½ teaspoons snipped fresh or ½ tea- spoon dried oregano leaves
1 teaspoon snipped fresh or ¼ teaspoon dried basil leaves
Grated Parmesan cheese

Remove any excess fat from chicken. Heat shortening in 12-inch skillet until melted. Coat chicken with flour. Cook chicken in shortening over medium-high heat 15 to 20 minutes or until brown; drain on paper towels.

Cut bell pepper and onions crosswise into halves; cut each half into fourths. Stir bell pep- per, onions and remaining ingredients except Parmesan cheese into skillet. Cover and simmer 30 to 40 minutes or until thickest pieces of chicken are done. Serve with Parmesan cheese.

6 servings

PER SERVING: Calories 400; Protein 31 g; Carbohy- drate 19 g; Fat 22 g; Cholesterol 85 mg; Sodium 720 mg

Tarragon Chicken

The subtle anise flavor and fragrance of fresh tarragon make this chicken dish a favorite in the Burgundy region of France.

2½- to 3-pound broiler-fryer chicken, cut up
1 cup chicken broth or bouillon
3 medium carrots, sliced
1 tablespoon snipped fresh or
    1 teaspoon dried tarragon leaves
1½ teaspoons salt
⅛ teaspoon pepper
1 bay leaf
4 ounces mushrooms, sliced
2 stalks celery, sliced
1 medium onion, sliced
½ cup dry white wine or chicken broth
½ cup half-and-half
3 tablespoons all-purpose flour
1 egg yolk
Hot cooked noodles

Heat chicken, chicken broth, carrots, tarragon, salt, pepper and bay leaf to boiling in 12-inch skillet or Dutch oven; reduce heat. Cover and simmer 30 minutes. Add mushrooms, celery and onion. Heat to boiling; reduce heat. Cover and simmer until thickest pieces of chicken are done, about 15 minutes.

Remove chicken and vegetables to warm platter with slotted spoon; keep warm. Drain liquid from skillet; strain and reserve 1 cup. Pour reserved liquid and the wine into skillet. Mix half-and-half, flour and egg yolk until smooth; stir into wine mixture. Cook, stirring constantly, until thickened. Serve with chicken, vegetables and noodles. **8 servings**

PER SERVING: Calories 370; Protein 30 g; Carbohydrate 31 g; Fat 14 g; Cholesterol 140 mg; Sodium 770 mg

Chicken Vindaloo

Dishes called "vindaloo" have a mixed heritage—Indian and Portuguese. Vindaloo means "wine-garlic" and refers to a marinade of wine or vinegar and garlic.

3 pounds chicken legs, thighs, and
    breast halves
¼ cup vinegar
2 tablespoons molasses
2 teaspoons ground turmeric
2 teaspoons ground coriander
1 teaspoon ground cumin
1 teaspoon chili powder
½ teaspoon dry mustard
2 cloves garlic, finely chopped
3 or 4 small jalapeño peppers,
    seeded and finely chopped
1 large onion, finely chopped (about 1
    cup)
½ teaspoon crushed red pepper
2 tablespoons vegetable oil
2 large tomatoes, chopped
9 new potatoes (about 1 pound), cooked
    and cut into halves
Chopped fresh cilantro

Remove skin from chicken. Mix vinegar, molasses, turmeric, coriander, cumin, chili powder, mustard, garlic and jalapeño peppers. Pour into shallow glass dish. Add chicken; turn to coat all sides. Cover and refrigerate at least 12 hours.

Cook and stir onion and red pepper in oil in 12-inch skillet over medium heat until onion is light brown. Add tomatoes; cook and stir until tomatoes are very soft, 5 to 7 minutes. Add chicken and marinade; cook uncovered over high heat, turning chicken occasionally, 10 minutes. Reduce heat; cover and simmer 15 minutes. Add potatoes; cover and simmer until thickest pieces of chicken are done, 10 to 15 minutes longer. Sprinkle with cilantro. **6 servings**

PER SERVING: Calories 370; Protein 33 g; Carbohydrate 32 g; Fat 12 g; Cholesterol 90 mg; Sodium 110 mg

Quick Barbecued Chicken Wings

2 pounds chicken drummettes
½ cup chili sauce
1 tablespoon honey
1 tablespoon soy sauce
½ teaspoon dry mustard
¼ teaspoon ground red pepper
   (cayenne)

Place drummettes in 10-inch nonstick skillet. Mix remaining ingredients; spoon over drummettes. Heat to boiling; reduce heat. Cover and cook over medium-low heat 20 to 25 minutes, stirring occasionally, until chicken is done.

4 servings

PER SERVING: Calories 305; Protein 23 g; Carbohydrate 13 g; Fat 18 g; Cholesterol 75 mg; Sodium 690 mg

Creamed Chicken Livers on Toast

2 tablespoons vegetable oil
8 ounces chicken livers, cut into fourths
4 ounces fresh mushrooms,* sliced
   (about
   1½ cups)
¼ cup chopped onion (about 1 small)
½ cup chicken bouillon
1 tablespoon all-purpose flour
1 teaspoon snipped fresh or ¼ teaspoon
   dried marjoram leaves
½ teaspoon salt
½ cup sour cream
4 slices bread, toasted and cut diagonally into halves

Heat oil in 10-inch skillet over medium heat until hot. Cook livers in oil about 4 minutes, stirring occasionally, until brown. Push to side of skillet. Cook and stir mushrooms and onion in skillet about 3 minutes or until onion is tender.

Shake bouillon, flour, marjoram and salt in tightly covered container; stir into skillet. Heat to boiling, stirring constantly. Boil and stir 1 minute; remove from heat. Stir in sour cream. Serve over toast triangles. **4 servings**

PER SERVING: Calories 260; Protein 13 g; Carbohydrate 18 g; Fat 15 g; Cholesterol 240 mg; Sodium 520 mg

*1 can (4 ounces) mushroom stems and pieces, drained, can be substituted for the fresh mushrooms.

4

Enticing Oven Entrées

Roast Chicken with Herbs

Wonderful for Sunday dinner.

2 tablespoons margarine or butter
2 tablespoons olive or vegetable oil
¼ cup finely chopped onion (about 1
   small)
¼ cup lemon juice
2 tablespoons Worcestershire sauce
1½ teaspoons snipped fresh or
   ½ teaspoon dried basil leaves
¾ teaspoon snipped fresh or ¼
   teaspoon dried marjoram leaves
¾ teaspoon snipped fresh or
   ¼ teaspoon dried oregano leaves
2 large cloves garlic, finely chopped
2½- to 3-pound broiler-fryer chicken,
   cut up

Heat margarine and oil in rectangular pan, 13 × 9 × 2 inches, in 375° oven until margarine is melted. Stir in remaining ingredients except chicken. Place chicken, skin sides up, in pan, turning to coat with herb mixture. Bake uncovered 30 minutes. Turn chicken; bake uncovered until thickest pieces are done, about 30 minutes longer. **7 servings**

PER SERVING: Calories 220; Protein 19 g; Carbohydrate 2 g; Fat 15 g; Cholesterol 60 mg; Sodium 140 mg

MICROWAVE DIRECTIONS: Place margarine and oil in rectangular microwavable dish, 12 × 7½ × 2 inches. Microwave uncovered on high until margarine is melted, 45 to 60 seconds. Stir in remaining ingredients except chicken. Place chicken in dish, turning to coat with herb mixture. Arrange chicken, skin sides up and thickest parts to outside edges, in dish. Cover with waxed paper and microwave on high 10 minutes; rotate dish ½ turn. Microwave until thickest pieces are done, 6 to 10 minutes.

Gingered Chicken with Pea Pods

2½- to 3-pound whole boiler-fryer chicken
¼ cup margarine or butter, melted
¼ teaspoon paprika
¼ teaspoon ground ginger
8 ounces fresh Chinese pea pods or 2 packages (6 ounces each) frozen Chinese pea pods
1 medium onion, cut into thin wedges
½ teaspoon ground turmeric
¼ teaspoon ground ginger
2 tablespoons margarine or butter
8 ounces medium mushrooms
1 teaspoon salt
2 teaspoons lemon juice
8 cherry tomatoes, cut into halves

Heat oven to 375°. Fold wings of chicken across back with tips touching. Tie drumsticks to tail. Place chicken, breast side up, on rack in shallow roasting pan. Mix ¼ cup margarine, the paprika and ¼ teaspoon ginger; generously brush over chicken. Roast uncovered, brushing with margarine mixture 2 or 3 times, until thickest parts are done, about 1¼ hours.

About 15 minutes before chicken is done, rinse frozen pea pods with cold water to separate; drain. Cook and stir onion, turmeric and ¼ teaspoon ginger in 2 tablespoons margarine in 10-inch skillet over medium heat until onion is almost tender, about 3 minutes.

Stir in pea pods, mushrooms, salt and lemon juice. Cook uncovered, stirring occasionally, until pea pods are hot, about 5 minutes. Stir in tomatoes; heat just until hot. Serve vegetables with chicken.   **7 servings**

PER SERVING: Calories 270; Protein 21 g; Carbohydrate 6 g; Fat 18 g; Cholesterol 60 mg; Sodium 480 mg

MICROWAVE DIRECTIONS: Prepare chicken for roasting as directed. Place chicken, breast side down, in square microwavable dish, 8 × 8 × 2 inches. Microwave uncovered on high 12 minutes.

Turn chicken, breast side up. Decrease ¼ cup melted margarine to 2 tablespoons. Mix melted margarine, paprika and ¼ teaspoon ginger; brush over chicken. Microwave uncovered until drumstick meat feels very soft when pressed between fingers, 10 to 14 minutes. Cover and keep warm.

Rinse frozen pea pods as directed. Mix onion, turmeric, ¼ teaspoon ginger and 2 tablespoons margarine in 1½-quart microwavable casserole. Cover tightly and microwave on high until onion is tender, 2 to 4 minutes; add pea pods, mushrooms, salt and lemon juice. Cover tightly and microwave until pea pods are tender, 4 to 7 minutes. Stir in tomatoes; let stand uncovered 3 minutes. Serve vegetables with chicken.

Carving Chicken

Gently pulling leg away from body, cut through joint between thigh and body. Remove leg. Cut between drumstick and thigh; slice off meat. Make a deep horizontal cut into breast just above wing. Insert fork in top of breast and, starting halfway up breast, carve thin slices down to the cut, working upward.

Gingered Chicken with Pea Pods

Lemon-Basil Chicken

Covering the chicken during the first hour of baking makes for a moist bird and keeps the basil from turning black.

3-pound broiler-fryer chicken
1 lemon
1 clove garlic, thinly sliced
½ cup snipped fresh or 1 tablespoon dried basil leaves
½ teaspoon garlic powder

Heat oven to 375°. Remove excess fat from chicken; fasten neck skin of chicken to back with skewer. Fold wings across back with tips touching. Grate 2 teaspoons lemon peel; reserve. Cut lemon into halves; rub chicken with juice from 1 lemon half. Place garlic, 2 tablespoons of the fresh basil (1 teaspoon dried basil leaves) and remaining lemon half in cavity. Rub chicken with reserved lemon peel; sprinkle garlic powder and remaining basil over chicken.

Place chicken, breast side up, on rack in shallow rectangular roasting pan. Cover and bake 1 hour. Uncover and bake until drumstick meat feels very soft when pressed between fingers, about 30 minutes longer. **4 servings**

PER SERVING: Calories 245; Protein 28 g; Carbohydrate 2 g; Fat 14 g; Cholesterol 90 mg; Sodium 80 mg

Spicy Peanut Chicken

2½-to 3-pound cut-up broiler-fryer chicken, skinned
⅓ cup peanut butter
1 tablespoon honey
3 tablespoons lime juice
2 tablespoons soy sauce
½ teaspoon ground cumin
½ teaspoon ground coriander
¼ teaspoon red pepper sauce
3 cups hot cooked rice
2 tablespoons sliced green onion tops or 1 tablespoon chopped fresh parsley

Place chicken in rectangular baking dish, 11 × 7 × 1½ inches. Mix peanut butter and honey. Gradually stir in lime juice and soy sauce. Stir in cumin, coriander and pepper sauce. Brush chicken with about half of the peanut butter mixture. Turn chicken; brush with remaining mixture. Cover and refrigerate at least 2 hours.

Heat oven to 375°. Cover and bake chicken, meaty sides up, 30 minutes; spoon sauce over chicken. Cover and bake about 20 minutes longer or until thickest pieces of chicken are done. Serve chicken over rice. Skim fat from drippings; spoon drippings over chicken. Sprinkle with onion tops. **6 servings**

PER SERVING: Calories 425; Protein 36 g; Carbohydrate 35 g; Fat 15 g; Cholesterol 90 mg; Sodium 890 mg

Baked Chicken with Biscuits and Gravy

A convenient one-dish dinner.

2½- to 3-pound broiler-fryer chicken,
   cut up
1 envelope (about 1½ ounces) onion
   soup mix
1 can (10¾ ounces) condensed
   cream of mushroom soup
⅔ cup water
1 can (4 ounces) mushroom stems
   and pieces, drained
2 cups Bisquick® Original baking mix
⅔ cup milk
1 teaspoon parsley flakes
Paprika

Heat oven to 400°. Place chicken, skin sides up, in ungreased baking pan, 13 × 9 × 2 inches. Reserve 2 tablespoons onion soup mix (dry). Mix remaining soup mix, the mushroom soup and water; pour over chicken. Cover and bake 1 hour. Spoon mushrooms over chicken. Mix baking mix, milk, reserved onion soup mix and the parsley flakes until soft dough forms; beat vigorously 30 seconds. Drop dough by spoonfuls onto chicken and gravy; sprinkle with paprika. Bake uncovered until biscuits are light brown, about 12 minutes. **6 servings**

PER SERVING: Calories 430; Protein 28 g; Carbohydrate 34 g; Fat 20 g; Cholesterol 70 mg; Sodium 1710 mg

Chicken and Dressing Casserole

2 tablespoons vegetable oil
⅓ cup all-purpose flour
1 teaspoon salt
½ teaspoon paprika
¼ teaspoon pepper
2½- to 3-pound broiler-fryer chicken,
   cut up
1 can (10¾ ounces) condensed cream of
   chicken or cream of mushroom soup
6 cups soft bread cubes
1 cup milk
¾ cup chopped celery
1 medium onion, chopped (about ½ cup)
¼ cup margarine or butter, melted
1 teaspoon salt
½ teaspoon ground sage
½ teaspoon dried thyme leaves
¼ teaspoon pepper

Heat oven to 350°. Heat oil in 10-inch skillet until hot. Mix flour, 1 teaspoon salt, the paprika and ¼ teaspoon pepper; coat chicken. Cook chicken in oil over medium heat until brown, about 15 minutes. Place in ungreased 2½-quart casserole or rectangular baking dish, 13 × 9 × 2 inches. Pour soup over chicken.

Toss remaining ingredients. Mound mixture on chicken. Cover and bake until thickest pieces of chicken are done, 1 to 1¼ hours.

7 servings

PER SERVING: Calories 465; Protein 28 g; Carbohydrate 28 g; Fat 27 g; Cholesterol 75 mg; Sodium 1460 mg

Fried Chicken

The all-time best "finger food"!

½ **cup all-purpose flour**
1 **teaspoon paprika**
½ **teaspoon salt**
¼ **teaspoon pepper**
3- **to 3½-pound broiler-fryer chicken,
   cut up**
Vegetable oil

Mix flour, paprika, salt and pepper. Coat chicken with flour mixture.

Heat oil (¼ inch) in 12-inch skillet over medium-high heat. Cook chicken in oil about 10 minutes or until light brown on all sides; reduce heat. Cover tightly and simmer about 35 minutes, turning once or twice, until juices run clear. If skillet cannot be covered tightly, add 1 to 2 tablespoons water. Remove cover during last 5 minutes of cooking to crisp chicken.

6 servings

PER SERVING: Calories 385; Protein 29 g; Carbohydrate 7 g; Fat 26 g; Cholesterol 90 mg; Sodium 265 mg

BUTTERMILK FRIED CHICKEN: Increase flour to 1 cup, paprika to 2 teaspoons and salt to 1 teaspoon. Dip chicken into 1 cup buttermilk before coating with flour mixture.

MARYLAND FRIED CHICKEN: Coat chicken with flour mixture. Beat 2 eggs and 2 tablespoons water. Mix 2 cups cracker crumbs, dry bread crumbs or 1 cup cornmeal and ¼ teaspoon salt. Dip chicken into egg mixture. Coat with cracker-crumb mixture.

Barbecued Chicken

Real barbecue flavor without the trouble of grilling.

2½- **to 3-pound broiler-fryer chicken, cut
   up**
½ **cup all-purpose flour**
1 **teaspoon salt**
1 **teaspoon paprika**
¼ **teaspoon pepper**
¼ **cup butter or margarine**
Barbecue Sauce (below)

Heat oven to 425°. Remove any excess fat from chicken. Mix flour, salt, paprika and pepper. Coat chicken with flour mixture. Heat butter in rectangular baking dish, 13 × 9 × 2 inches, in oven until melted. Place chicken pieces, skin sides down, in dish. Bake 45 minutes; drain fat from dish and turn chicken. Reduce oven temperature to 375°. Prepare Barbecue Sauce. Spoon hot Barbecue Sauce over chicken. Bake 15 minutes or until thickest pieces are done.

4 to 6 servings

PER SERVING: Calories 525; Protein 37 g; Carbohydrate 34 g; Fat 27 g; Cholesterol 135 mg; Sodium 1990 mg

Barbecue Sauce

1 **cup ketchup or 1 can (8 ounces) tomato sauce**
½ **cup hot water**
⅓ **cup lemon juice**
1 **teaspoon salt**
1 **teaspoon sugar**
2 **teaspoons paprika**
½ **teaspoon pepper**
1 **tablespoon Worcestershire sauce**
1 **medium onion, finely chopped (about
   ½ cup)**

Heat all ingredients to boiling, stirring occasionally.

Barbecued Chicken

Oven-fried Chicken

Save splatters—and calories—with this delicious "fried" chicken.

¼ **cup margarine or butter**
½ **cup all-purpose flour**
1 **teaspoon paprika**
½ **teaspoon salt**
¼ **teaspoon pepper**
3-**pound broiler-fryer chicken, cut up**

Heat oven to 425°. Heat margarine in rectangular pan, 13 × 9 × 2 inches, in oven until melted. Mix flour, paprika, salt and pepper. Coat chicken with flour mixture. Place chicken, skin sides down, in pan. Bake uncovered 30 minutes. Turn chicken and bake about 30 minutes longer or until juices run clear.   **6 servings**

PER SERVING: Calories 350; Protein 29 g; Carbohydrate 7 g; Fat 22 g; Cholesterol 90 mg; Sodium 355 mg

CRUNCHY OVEN-FRIED CHICKEN: Substitute 1 cup cornflake crumbs for the ½ cup flour. Dip chicken into ¼ cup margarine or butter, melted, before coating with crumb mixture.

PER SERVING: Calories 350; Protein 29 g; Carbohydrate 8 g; Fat 22 g; Cholesterol 90 mg; Sodium 455 mg

Zesty Chicken Oregano

Olive oil, garlic and lemon are flavors basic to many Greek foods, as well as the oregano in this baked chicken.

2½ **to 3-pound broiler-fryer chicken, cut up**
½ **cup olive or vegetable oil**
¼ **cup lemon juice**
2 **teaspoons dried oregano leaves**
1 **teaspoon salt**
½ **teaspoon pepper**
1 **clove garlic, chopped**
Lemon slices

Heat oven to 375°. Place chicken in ungreased oblong pan, 13 × 9 × 2 inches. Mix remaining ingredients except lemon slices; pour over chicken. Bake uncovered, spooning oil mixture over chicken occasionally, 30 minutes. Turn chicken; cook until thickest pieces are done, about 30 minutes longer. Garnish with lemon slices.   **6 to 8 servings**

PER SERVING: Calories 350; Protein 23 g; Carbohydrate 2 g; Fat 28 g; Cholesterol 70 mg; Sodium 420 mg

---

Quick Chicken Coating

For no-mess chicken coating, simply mix flour and seasonings in a plastic or paper bag. Shake the chicken, 2 or 3 pieces at a time, in the bag until evenly coated with the flour mixture. For added flavor, try adding a dash of one of the following spices to the flour:

• cayenne pepper
• garlic powder
• chili powder
• curry powder
• dill weed
• cumin
• rosemary

Country Captain

The history of this dish is cloaked in mystery. How did Indian spices find their way into fried chicken? Georgians claim a spice-trading captain brought the recipe to Savannah. But the recipe also may have evolved when English traders were stationed in East India.

2½- to 3-pound broiler-fryer chicken,
  cut up
½ cup all-purpose flour
1 teaspoon salt
¼ teaspoon pepper
¼ cup vegetable oil
1½ teaspoons curry powder
1½ teaspoons snipped fresh or
  ½ teaspoon dried thyme leaves
¼ teaspoon salt
1 large onion, chopped (about 1 cup)
1 green bell pepper, chopped
1 clove garlic, finely chopped, or
  ⅛ teaspoon garlic powder
1 can (16 ounces) whole tomatoes;
  undrained
¼ cup currants or raisins
⅓ cup slivered almonds, toasted
3 cups hot cooked rice

Heat oven to 350°. Remove any excess fat from chicken. Mix flour, 1 teaspoon salt and the pepper. Coat chicken with flour mixture. Heat oil in 10-inch skillet until hot. Cook chicken in oil over medium heat 15 to 20 minutes or until light brown. Place chicken in ungreased 2½-quart casserole. Drain oil from skillet. Add curry powder, thyme, ¼ teaspoon salt, the onion, bell pepper, garlic and tomatoes to skillet. Heat to boiling, stirring frequently, to loosen brown particles from skillet. Pour over chicken. Cover and bake about 40 minutes or until thickest pieces are done. Skim fat from liquid if necessary; add currants. Bake uncovered 5 minutes. Sprinkle with almonds. Serve with rice and, if desired, grated fresh coconut and chutney.

6 servings

PER SERVING: Calories 530; Protein 29 g; Carbohydrate 50 g; Fat 24 g; Cholesterol 70 mg; Sodium 700 mg

Apricot Chicken

3-pound broiler-fryer chicken,
  cut up and skinned
2 tablespoons soy sauce
2 tablespoons honey
1 tablespoon vegetable oil
1 tablespoon chili sauce
½ teaspoon ground ginger
⅛ teaspoon ground red pepper (cayenne)
1 can (16 ounces) apricot halves in juice,
  drained

Heat oven in 375°. Remove excess fat from chicken. Place chicken, meaty sides up, in rectangular pan, 13 × 9 × 2 inches. Mix remaining ingredients except apricots; brush over chicken, turning pieces to coat. Bake uncovered, brushing with soy mixture occasionally, until thickest pieces are done, 50 to 60 minutes. About 5 minutes before chicken is done, arrange apricots around chicken; brush chicken and apricots with soy mixture. Bake until apricots are hot, about 5 minutes.

6 servings

PER SERVING: Calories 205; Protein 23 g; Carbohydrate 17 g; Fat 5 g; Cholesterol 60 mg Sodium 430 mg

MICROWAVE DIRECTIONS: Prepare soy mixture as directed. Arrange chicken, meaty sides up, thickest parts to outside edges, in rectangular microwavable dish, 12 × 7½ × 2 inches. Brush chicken with soy mixture, turning pieces to coat. Cover tightly and microwave on high 10 minutes. Brush with soy mixture; rotate dish ½ turn. Cover tightly and microwave until thickest pieces are done, 6 to 10 minutes longer. Arrange apricots around chicken; brush chicken and apricots with soy mixture. Microwave uncovered until apricots are hot, about 1 minute.

Moroccan Chicken with Olives

Moroccan Chicken with Olives

Lemon sharpens the spicy sauce of this Moroccan specialty.

¼ cup snipped fresh cilantro
1 tablespoon paprika
2 teaspoons ground cumin
½ teaspoon salt
½ teaspoon ground turmeric
½ teaspoon ground ginger
2 cloves garlic, finely chopped
3- to 3½-pound broiler-fryer chicken, cut up
⅓ cup all-purpose flour
½ cup water
¼ cup lemon juice
1 teaspoon instant chicken bouillon
½ cup Kalamata or Green olives
1 lemon, sliced

Heat oven to 350°. Mix cilantro, paprika, cumin, salt, turmeric, ginger and garlic. Rub mixture on all sides of chicken; coat with flour. Place chicken in ungreased oblong baking dish, 13 × 9 × 2 inches. Mix water, lemon juice and bouillon (dry); pour over chicken. Add olives and lemon slices. Bake uncovered, spooning juices over chicken occasionally, until thickest pieces of chicken are done, about 1 hour. Serve with couscous or rice if desired.

6 servings

PER SERVING: Calories 265; Protein 28 g; Carbohydrate 9 g; Fat 13 g; Cholesterol 85 mg; Sodium 370 mg

Crunchy Almond Chicken

1 cup blanched slivered almonds
1 clove garlic
1 thin slice gingerroot
1 teaspoon salt
1 teaspoon paprika
¼ teaspoon ground cumin
¼ teaspoon pepper
2½- to 3-pound broiler-fryer chicken, cut up
⅓ cup margarine or butter, melted

Place almonds, garlic and gingerroot in blender container; cover and blend until finely ground. Mix almond mixture, salt, paprika, cumin and pepper. Dip chicken into margarine; roll in almond mixture. Place chicken, skin sides up, in ungreased oblong pan, 13 × 9 × 2 inches. Bake uncovered until thickest pieces are done, 55 to 60 minutes.

8 servings

PER SERVING: Calories 400; Protein 27 g; Carbohydrate 5 g; Fat 30 g; Cholesterol 70 mg; Sodium 540 mg

Substituting Chicken Parts

Your favorite chicken pieces can be used in any of the recipes calling for a cut-up broiler-fryer chicken—just substitute 2 to 2½ pounds pieces. Remember, while drumsticks, thighs and breasts may cost more per pound, they have a higher yield of edible meat. And you get just what you like in the bargain!

Five-Spice Chicken

The five spices used in our recipe are similar to the traditional spices called for in Chinese dishes. Five-spice powders may contain, in addition to the spices below, fennel seed, Sichuan peppers or star anise.

2½- to 3-pound broiler-fryer chicken,
   cut up
⅓ cup soy sauce
2 tablespoons vegetable oil
1 small onion, chopped
1 clove garlic, finely chopped
½ teaspoon ground ginger
¼ teaspoon ground cinnamon
¼ teaspoon crushed anise seed
⅛ teaspoon ground nutmeg
⅛ teaspoon ground cloves

Place chicken in shallow glass or plastic dish. Mix remaining ingredients; pour over chicken. Cover and refrigerate, spooning marinade over chicken occasionally, at least 1 hour.

Heat oven to 350°. Remove chicken from marinade; reserve marinade. Place chicken in ungreased oblong baking dish, 12 × 7½ × 2 inches. Brush marinade on chicken. Bake uncovered, brushing once or twice with marinade, until thickest pieces of chicken are done, about 1 hour. **8 servings**

PER SERVING: Calories 230; Protein 23 g; Carbohydrate 23 g; Fat 14 g; Cholesterol 70 mg; Sodium 970 mg

Grilled Tarragon Chicken Bundles

6 skinless boneless chicken breast
   halves (about 1½ pounds)
6 medium carrots, cut lengthwise into
   quarters, then into 3-inch pieces
4 ounces mushrooms
6 small zucchini, cut lengthwise into quarters, then into 3-inch pieces
½ cup margarine or butter, melted
1 tablespoon snipped fresh or
   1 teaspoon dried tarragon leaves
1 teaspoon salt
¼ teaspoon pepper

Place chicken breast half on each of 6 pieces heavy-duty aluminum foil, 18 × 14 inches; top with vegetables. Drizzle with margarine; sprinkle with tarragon, salt and pepper. Wrap securely with foil.

Grill bundles 5 to 6 inches from hot coals until chicken is done and vegetables are tender, 45 to 60 minutes. **6 servings**

PER SERVING: Calories 325; Protein 27 g; Carbohydrate 12 g; Fat 19 g; Cholesterol 60 mg; Sodium 620 mg

TO BAKE: Bake bundles in shallow pan in 350° oven until chicken is done and vegetables are tender, 50 to 60 minutes.

Grilled Tarragon Chicken Bundles

Chicken Rolls with Pork Stuffing

3 large whole chicken breasts
(about 3 pounds), boned,
skinned and cut into halves
½ pound ground pork
1 small onion, finely chopped
1 clove garlic, chopped
½ cup soft bread crumbs
½ teaspoon salt
¼ teaspoon ground savory
¼ teaspoon pepper
1 egg, beaten
2 tablespoons margarine or
butter, melted
½ teaspoon salt
½ cup dry white wine or chicken broth
½ cup cold water
2 teaspoons cornstarch
½ teaspoon instant chicken
bouillon
Snipped parsley

Heat oven to 400°. Place chicken between 2 pieces of waxed paper or plastic wrap; pound until ¼ inch thick, being careful not to tear chicken.

Cook and stir pork, onion and garlic over medium heat until pork is brown. Drain fat. Stir bread crumbs, ½ teaspoon salt, the savory, pepper and egg into pork mixture. Place about ⅓ cup pork mixture on each chicken breast half. Roll up; secure with wooden picks. Place rolls in greased rectangular baking dish, 11 × 7 × 1½ inches. Brush rolls with margarine; pour any remaining margarine over rolls. Sprinkle with ½ teaspoon salt; add wine. Bake uncovered until chicken is done, 35 to 40 minutes.

Remove chicken to warm platter; remove wooden picks. Keep chicken warm. Pour liquid from baking dish into 1-quart saucepan. Stir water into cornstarch; pour into liquid. Stir in

bouillon (dry). Heat to boiling over medium heat, stirring constantly. Boil and stir 1 minute. Pour gravy over chicken; sprinkle with parsley. Serve with spinach noodles if desired.

6 servings

PER SERVING: Calories 430; Protein 58 g; Carbohydrate 9 g; Fat 18 g; Cholesterol 185 mg; Sodium 600 mg

Chicken Teriyaki

2 small whole chicken breasts
(about 1 pound), boned, skinned and
cut into halves
¼ cup soy sauce
¼ cup vegetable oil
2 tablespoons white wine*
2 teaspoons chopped gingerroot or
½ teaspoon ground ginger
1 teaspoon sugar
1 clove garlic, finely chopped

Place chicken in glass or plastic container. Mix remaining ingredients; pour over chicken. Cover and refrigerate, turning occasionally, at least 1 hour.

Set over control to broil and/or 550°. Place chicken on rack in broiler pan. Broil with tops about 4 inches from heat 5 minutes; turn chicken. Brush with marinade; broil until chicken is done, 5 to 6 minutes longer. Place on warm platter. Serve with cooked rice, if desired.

4 servings

PER SERVING: Calories 165; Protein 25 g; Carbohydrate 1 g; Fat 7 g; Cholesterol 60 mg; Sodium 310 mg

*Apple juice, pineapple juice, orange juice or water can be substituted for the wine.

Tropical Chicken Rolls

A zesty dish with the great flavors of the tropics.

4 large skinless boneless chicken
    breast halves (about 1½ pounds)
1 large red bell pepper, finely
    chopped
3 tablespoons grated Parmesan
    cheese
2 tablespoons pine nuts, chopped
1 tablespoon olive or vegetable oil
⅛ teaspoon salt
⅛ teaspoon pepper
1 clove garlic, chopped
½ cup flaked or shredded coconut
2 tablespoons sliced green
    onions (with tops)
2 tablespoons snipped fresh
    cilantro
1 tablespoon finely chopped
    gingerroot
2 tablespoons lime juice
1 large mango, pared and chopped
1 large papaya, pared, seeded
    and chopped
1 jalapeño chili, seeded and
    finely chopped

Flatten each chicken breast to ¼-inch thickness between plastic wrap. Mix bell pepper, cheese, pine nuts, oil, salt, pepper and garlic. Spread ¼ of bell pepper mixture on each of the chicken breasts. Roll tightly; secure with toothpicks.

Set oven control to broil. Place chicken, seam sides down, on rack in broiler pan. Broil 4 to 5 inches from heat 25 to 30 minutes or until done. Remove toothpicks. Mix remaining ingredients; serve with chicken. **4 servings**

PER SERVING: Calories 425; Protein 44 g; Carbohydrate 37 g; Fat 13 g; Cholesterol 100 mg; Sodium 370 mg

Tandoori-style Chicken

Chicken with a taste of India.

8 chicken breast halves (about 4
    pounds), skinned and boned
½ teaspoon water
¼ teaspoon dry mustard
1 cup plain yogurt
¼ cup lemon juice
1½ teaspoons salt
1½ teaspoons paprika
½ teaspoon ground cardamom
½ teaspoon each red and yellow food
    color, if desired
¼ teaspoon ground ginger
¼ teaspoon ground cumin
¼ teaspoon crushed red pepper
¼ teaspoon pepper
1 clove garlic, crushed

Heat oven to 375°. Place chicken in glass bowl. Mix water and mustard; stir in remaining ingredients. Pour over chicken; turn to coat well. Cover and refrigerate at least 12 hours but no longer than 24 hours. Remove chicken from marinade; place chicken in ungreased baking dish, 13 × 9 × 2 inches. Bake uncovered until done, about 45 minutes. **8 servings**

PER SERVING: Calories 255; Protein 49 g; Carbohydrate 1 g; Fat 6 g; Cholesterol 125 mg; Sodium 220 mg

Honey-Ginger Chicken

2 tablespoons vegetable oil
2 tablespoons margarine or butter
⅓ cup all-purpose flour
1½ teaspoons grated gingerroot or
    ½ teaspoon ground ginger
¼ teaspoon pepper
3 pounds chicken drumsticks or thighs
⅓ cup honey
⅓ cup chili sauce
⅓ cup soy sauce
½ teaspoon ground ginger

Heat oven to 425°. Heat oil and margarine in rectangular pan, 13 × 9 × 2 inches, in oven until melted. Mix flour, 1½ teaspoons gingerroot and the pepper. Coat chicken pieces thoroughly with flour mixture. Place chicken, skin sides down, in pan. Bake uncovered 30 minutes. Turn chicken; bake 15 minutes. Remove chicken and drain fat. Line pan with aluminum foil. Return chicken to pan.

Mix remaining ingredients. Pour over chicken. Bake 15 minutes, spooning honey mixture over chicken every 5 minutes, until juices run clear.

6 servings

PER SERVING: Calories 500; Protein 42 g; Carbohydrate 25 g; Fat 29 g; Cholesterol 145 mg; Sodium 1285 mg

MICROWAVE DIRECTIONS: Omit oil and margarine. Coat chicken pieces as directed. Arrange chicken, skin sides up and thickest parts to outside edges, in rectangular microwavable dish, 13 × 9 × 2 inches. Cover with waxed paper and microwave on high 10 minutes; drain. Mix remaining ingredients. Pour over chicken. Cover with waxed paper and microwave on high 10 to 15 minutes, rotating dish ½ turn every 5 minutes and spooning sauce over chicken, until juices run clear.

Chicken with Black Beans

4 chicken drumsticks (about 1 pound)
4 chicken thighs (about 1 pound)
2 cans (15 ounces each) black beans, undrained
1 tablespoon grated gingerroot or 1 teaspoon ground ginger
1 teaspoon finely shredded lime peel
2 tablespoons lime juice
½ teaspoon salt
1 clove garlic, finely chopped
1 cup cubed mango (about 1 medium) or 1 can (8 ounces) peach slices, drained and cut up
¼ cup thinly sliced green onions with tops (about 2 medium)

Heat oven to 375°. Place chicken pieces, skin sides up, in ungreased rectangular baking dish, 13 × 9 × 2 inches. Bake uncovered 40 minutes. Remove excess fat. Mix remaining ingredients. Spoon around chicken pieces. Cover and bake 30 minutes longer or until juices of chicken run clear.

4 servings

PER SERVING: Calories 310; Protein 28 g; Carbohydrate 22 g; Fat 12 g; Cholesterol 80 mg; Sodium 210 mg

Chicken with Black Beans

Spicy Drumsticks with Blue Cheese Sauce

It is hard to believe these drumsticks are guilt-free. The Blue Cheese Sauce also makes a superb dip for vegetables or salad dressing.

Blue Cheese Sauce (below)
1 tablespoon vegetable oil
1 tablespoon vinegar
1 to 2 teaspoons red pepper sauce
¼ teaspoon salt
12 chicken drumsticks (about 2 pounds)

Prepare Blue Cheese Sauce. Mix oil, vinegar, pepper sauce and salt in glass or plastic bowl or heavy plastic bag; add drumsticks and toss until evenly coated. Cover and refrigerate at least 1 hour.

Set oven control to broil. Place chicken on rack sprayed with nonstick cooking spray in broiler pan. Broil with tops about 6 inches from heat 20 minutes. Turn; broil until chicken is done, 15 to 20 minutes longer. Serve with Blue Cheese Sauce.   **6 servings**

PER SERVING: Calories 310; Protein 33 g; Carbohydrate 4 g; Fat 18 g; Cholesterol 110 mg; Sodium 320 mg

Blue Cheese Sauce

1 cup nonfat plain yogurt.
2 tablespoons finely crumbled blue cheese (1 ounce)
2 tablespoons reduced-calorie mayonnaise or salad dressing
½ teaspoon celery seed

Mix all ingredients; cover and refrigerate 1 hour.

Glazed Chicken Drumsticks

12 chicken drumsticks (about 2 pounds)
3 tablespoons soy sauce
2 tablespoons honey
1 tablespoon vegetable oil
1 tablespoon chili sauce
½ teaspoon salt
¼ teaspoon ground ginger
⅛ teaspoon garlic powder

Place chicken drumsticks in ungreased shallow glass dish. Mix remaining ingredients; pour over chicken. Cover and refrigerate at least 1 hour.

Heat oven to 375°. Line broiler pan with aluminum foil. Place chicken on rack in broiler pan. Brush chicken with remaining sauce. Bake 50 to 60 minutes or until done.   **6 servings**

PER SERVING: Calories 295; Protein 30 g; Carbohydrate 7 g; Fat 15 g; Cholesterol 125 mg; Sodium 860 mg

Blue Cornmeal Chicken Wings

Try serving small portions as appetizers.

¼ cup lime juice
¼ cup vegetable oil
½ teaspoon crushed red pepper
10 chicken wings (about
  2 pounds)
2 tablespoons margarine or
  butter
½ cup blue or yellow cornmeal
2 tablespoons all-purpose flour
½ teaspoon salt
½ teaspoon ground cumin
⅛ teaspoon pepper

Mix lime juice, oil and red pepper in large glass or plastic bowl. Separate chicken wings at joints; discard tips. Cut off and discard excess skin. Place chicken in oil mixture; stir to coat. Cover and refrigerate at least 3 hours, stirring occasionally; drain.

Heat oven to 425°. Heat margarine in rectangular pan, 13 × 9 × 2 inches, in oven until melted. Shake remaining ingredients in plastic bag, or mix in bowl. Shake chicken in cornmeal mixture to coat; place in pan. Bake uncovered 20 minutes; turn chicken. Bake 20 to 25 minutes longer or until golden brown.

20 chicken wing pieces

PER SERVING: Calories 140; Protein 8 g; Carbohydrate 2 g; Fat 11 g; Cholesterol 35 mg; Sodium 105 mg

Do-ahead Sesame Chicken Wings

20 chicken wings (about
  4 pounds)
2 tablespoons margarine or
  butter, melted
1½ cups variety baking mix
½ cup sesame seed
2 teaspoons paprika
1½ teaspoons dry mustard
½ teaspoon salt
2 eggs
2 tablespoons milk
¼ cup margarine or butter,
  melted

Separate chicken wings at joints; discard tips. Spread 1 tablespoon margarine in each of 2 rectangular pans, 13 × 9 × 2 inches. Mix baking mix, sesame seed, paprika, mustard and salt. Beat eggs and milk with fork. Dip chicken into egg mixture; coat with sesame seed mixture. Arrange close together in pans. Cover and refrigerate up to 6 hours (or bake immediately).

Heat oven to 425°. Drizzle ¼ cup margarine over chicken. Bake uncovered 35 to 40 minutes or until brown and crisp.

40 chicken wing pieces

PER SERVING: Calories 150; Protein 9 g; Carbohydrate 3 g; Fat 11 g; Cholesterol 45 mg; Sodium 135 mg

Chicken Pot Pie

3 tablespoons butter or margarine
3 tablespoons all-purpose flour
½ teaspoon salt
1 teaspoon snipped fresh or ¼ teaspoon dried thyme leaves
⅛ teaspoon pepper
¾ cup chicken broth
¾ cup whipping cream
2 cups cooked chicken or turkey, cut into 1-inch pieces
1 package (10 ounces) frozen peas and carrots*
1 cup frozen or canned small whole onions
Pastry for 9-inch one-crust pie

Heat butter in 3-quart saucepan over low heat until melted. Stir in flour, salt, thyme and pepper. Cook, stirring constantly, until mixture is smooth and bubbly; remove from heat. Stir in broth and whipping cream. Heat to boiling, stirring constantly. Boil and stir 1 minute. Stir in chicken, peas and carrots and onions.

Heat oven to 425°. Prepare pastry. Roll ⅔ of the pastry into 12-inch square; fit into square baking dish, 8 × 8 × 2 inches. Pour chicken mixture into pastry-lined dish. Roll remaining pastry into rectangle, about 10 × 6 inches. Cut rectangle into 12 strips, each ½ inch wide.

Place 7 pastry strips across filling; arrange remaining strips crisscross to make lattice top. Trim; turn edge of bottom crust over strips. Seal and flute. Bake 35 to 40 minutes or until light brown.   **6 servings**

PER SERVING: Calories 750; Protein 35 g; Carbohydrate 42 g; Fat 49 g; Cholesterol 125 mg; Sodium 780 mg

Pastry

For a 9-inch one crust pie.

⅓ cup lard or ⅓ cup plus 1 tablespoon shortening
1 cup all-purpose flour
½ teaspoon salt
2 to 3 tablespoons cold water

Cut lard into flour and salt until particles are size of small peas. Sprinkle with water, 1 tablespoon at a time, tossing with fork until all flour is moistened and pastry almost cleans side of bowl (1 to 2 teaspoons water can be added if necessary).

*1 can (16 ounces) peas and carrots, drained, can be substituted for the frozen peas and carrots.

Chicken Pot Pie

Cheese and Chicken Pizza

Chicken makes a different, and very tasty, topping for pizza.

    1 can (8 ounces) tomato sauce
    1 teaspoon dried oregano
      leaves
    1/2 teaspoon dried basil leaves
    1/2 teaspoon salt
    1/4 teaspoon garlic or onion
      powder
    1/8 teaspoon pepper
    2 cups Bisquick® Original baking mix
    1/2 cup cold water
    1 1/2 cups shredded Monterey
      Jack cheese (about
      6 ounces)
    2 cups cut-up cooked chicken
    1/2 cup sliced ripe olives
    1 medium avocado
    Lemon juice

Heat oven to 425°. Mix tomato sauce, oregano, basil, salt, garlic powder and pepper; reserve. Mix baking mix and water until soft dough forms. Roll or pat dough into 12-inch circle on ungreased cookie sheet; pinch edge of circle, forming 1/2-inch rim.

Sprinkle 1/2 cup of the cheese over crust; spread tomato sauce mixture over top. Top with chicken and olives. Sprinkle with remaining cheese. Bake uncovered until crust is golden brown, 20 to 25 minutes. Cut avocado lengthwise into slices; sprinkle with lemon juice. Garnish pizza with avocado. **1 pizza**

PER SERVING: Calories 805; Protein 57 g; Carbohydrate 48 g; Fat 43 g; Cholesterol 155 mg; Sodium 1990 mg

Chicken-Cheese Lasagne

    1/2 cup margarine or butter
    2 cloves garlic, crushed
    1/2 cup all-purpose flour
    1 teaspoon salt
    2 cups milk
    2 cups chicken broth
    2 cups shredded mozzarella
      cheese (about 8 ounces)
    1/2 cup grated Parmesan cheese
    1 medium onion, chopped
      (about 1/2 cup)
    1 teaspoon dried basil leaves
    1/2 teaspoon dried oregano leaves
    1/4 teaspoon pepper
    8 ounces uncooked lasagne
      noodles (9 or 10 noodles)
    2 cups creamed cottage cheese
      (16 ounces)
    2 cups cut-up cooked chicken
    2 packages (10 ounces each)
      frozen chopped spinach,
      thawed and well drained
    1/2 cup grated Parmesan cheese

Heat oven to 350°. Heat margarine in 2-quart saucepan over low heat until melted; add garlic. Stir in flour and salt. Cook, stirring constantly, until bubbly. Remove from heat; stir in milk and broth. Heat to boiling, stirring constantly. Boil and stir 1 minute. Stir in mozzarella cheese, 1/2 cup Parmesan cheese, the onion, basil, oregano and pepper. Cook over low heat, stirring constantly, until mozzarella cheese is melted.

Spread 1/4 of the cheese sauce (about 1 1/2 cups) in ungreased rectangular baking dish, 13 × 9 × 2 inches; top with 3 or 4 uncooked noodles, overlapping if necessary. Spread half of the cottage cheese over noodles. Repeat with 1/4 of the cheese sauce, 3 or 4 noodles and remaining cottage cheese. Top with chicken, spinach, 1/4 of the cheese sauce, the remaining noodles and the remaining cheese sauce. Sprinkle with 1/2 cup Parmesan cheese. Bake uncovered until noodles are done, 35 to 40 minutes. Let stand 15 minutes before cutting. **12 servings**

PER SERVING: Calories 385; Protein 32 g; Carbohydrate 22 g; Fat 19 g; Cholesterol 60 mg; Sodium 850 mg

Chicken Quiche

Pastry (right)
1 cup cut-up cooked chicken
1 cup shredded natural Swiss cheese (about 4 ounces)
⅓ cup finely chopped onion
4 eggs
2 cups half-and-half
1 teaspoon salt
½ teaspoon dried thyme leaves
¼ teaspoon pepper

Heat oven to 425°. Prepare Pastry. Sprinkle chicken, cheese and onion in pastry-lined pie plate. Beat eggs slightly; beat in remaining ingredients. Pour into pie plate. Bake uncovered 15 minutes.

Reduce oven temperatures to 300°. Bake uncovered until knife inserted halfway between center and edge comes out clean, about 30 minutes. Let stand 10 minutes before cutting. **6 servings**

PER SERVING: Calories 500; Protein 28 g; Carbohydrate 21 g; Fat 34 g; Cholesterol 230 mg; Sodium 690 mg

Pastry

⅓ cup plus 1 tablespoon shortening or ⅓ cup lard
1 cup all-purpose flour
½ teaspoon salt
2 to 3 tablespoons cold water

Cut shortening into flour and salt until particles are size of small peas. Sprinkle in water, 1 tablespoon at a time, tossing with fork until all flour is moistened and pastry almost cleans side of bowl (1 to 2 teaspoons water can be added if necessary).

Gather pastry into a ball; shape into flattened round on lightly floured cloth-covered board. Roll pastry 2 inches larger than inverted pie plate, 9 × 1¼ inches, with floured stockinet-covering rolling pin. Fold pastry into quarters; unfold and ease into plate, pressing firmly against bottom and side. Trim overhanging edge of pastry 1 inch from rim of plate. Fold and roll pastry under, even with plate; flute.

DO-AHEAD NOTE: After sprinkling pastry with chicken, cheese and onion, cover and refrigerate. Beat remaining ingredients; cover and refrigerate. Store no longer than 24 hours. About 1 hour before serving, stir egg mixture and pour into pie plate. Continue as directed—except increase second baking time to about 45 minutes.

METRIC CONVERSION GUIDE

U.S. UNITS	CANADIAN METRIC	AUSTRALIAN METRIC
Volume		
1/4 teaspoon	1 mL	1 ml
1/2 teaspoon	2 mL	2 ml
1 teaspoon	5 mL	5 ml
1 tablespoon	15 mL	20 ml
1/4 cup	50 mL	60 ml
1/3 cup	75 mL	80 ml
1/2 cup	125 mL	125 ml
2/3 cup	150 mL	170 ml
3/4 cup	175 mL	190 ml
1 cup	250 mL	250 ml
1 quart	1 liter	1 liter
1 1/2 quarts	1.5 liter	1.5 liter
2 quarts	2 liters	2 liters
2 1/2 quarts	2.5 liters	2.5 liters
3 quarts	3 liters	3 liters
4 quarts	4 liters	4 liters
Weight		
1 ounce	30 grams	30 grams
2 ounces	55 grams	60 grams
3 ounces	85 grams	90 grams
4 ounces (1/4 pound)	115 grams	125 grams
8 ounces (1/2 pound)	225 grams	225 grams
16 ounces (1 pound)	455 grams	500 grams
1 pound	455 grams	1/2 kilogram

Measurements

Inches	Centimeters
1	2.5
2	5.0
3	7.5
4	10.0
5	12.5
6	15.0
7	17.5
8	20.5
9	23.0
10	25.5
11	28.0
12	30.5
13	33.0
14	35.5
15	38.0

Temperatures

Fahrenheit	Celsius
32°	0°
212°	100°
250°	120°
275°	140°
300°	150°
325°	160°
350°	180°
375°	190°
400°	200°
425°	220°
450°	230°
475°	240°
500°	260°

NOTE
The recipes in this cookbook have not been developed or tested using metric measures. When converting recipes to metric, some variations in quality may be noted.

Index